REFLECTIONS ON

Being Your True Self

IN ANY SITUATION

A Wise Inner Counselor Book

REFLECTIONS ON

Being Your True Self

IN ANY SITUATION

Cheryl Lafferty Eckl

FLYING CRANE PRESS

Published by Flying Crane Press, Livingston, Montana 59047
Cheryl@CherylEckl.com | www.CherylEckl.com

Select images and art not the author's own are used by permission of the artist or photographer; or are free stock images from pexels.com, pixabay.com, pixy.org, stocksnap.io; or from NASA.gov Hubble image gallery; or are royalty-free purchases of standard permitted use images through 123rf.com, istock.com, bigstockphoto.com.

The information and insights in this book are solely the opinion of the author and should not be considered as a form of therapy, advice, direction, diagnosis and/or treatment of any kind. This information is not a substitute for medical, psychological or other professional advice, counseling or care. All matters pertaining to your individual health should be supervised by a physician or appropriate healthcare practitioner. Neither the author nor the publisher assumes any responsibility or liability whatsoever on behalf of any purchaser or reader.

Library of Congress Control Number: 2021904186
ISBN: 978-1-7367123-0-6 (paperback)
ISBN: 978-1-7367123-1-3 (e-book)

Printed in the United States of America

To all who would be
their True Self

Dear Reader,

While reflecting upon how to begin this book, it occurred to me that I have been working on it for most of my life—which now stretches many decades beyond its beginning in a sleepy little town in the suburbs of Denver, Colorado.

That town is not so sleepy these days. But when I grew up there in a house my father built on a lot that had been part of an apple orchard, there were pheasants in the alfalfa field across our dirt road. Pigs and chickens lived at the tiny farm on the corner, and a herd of Aberdeen Angus cattle grazed peacefully on the other side of the main street with the rather ambitious name of Littleton Boulevard.

Life was quiet in those days. As an only child, I relished the silence of my home life and delighted in the peace I found as an avid reader. I would spend hours alone on my swing set or sitting in the gnarled old apple tree whose sturdy branches cradled my musings.

In those calming hours, I became well-acquainted with the inner presence that only years later I decided to call my Wise Inner Counselor™ and that I now know as my True Self.

I suppose I had to wander far afield from that inner guide before learning its value. If we do not pay attention, life in this world has a way of distracting us from what is most essential.

Anyway, that is what happened to me. Perhaps to you, as well.

These days I do not believe we can afford to ignore the inner voice. We can no longer assume that life will benignly carry us along to some happy conclusion. There are too many forces relentlessly determined to do exactly the opposite.

Fortunately, the True Self is stronger, wiser and more loving than the outer self—which for most of us is a false self that has developed from defense mechanisms or survival techniques rather than from a sense that there is more to us and life itself than the mere pursuit of the things of this world.

Life has pruned me of many desires and attachments to those

outer distractions. What remains is a longing to feel the presence of my True Self and to be that Self in any situation.

I want to make better use of this precious life I am living. I want to contribute more understanding to the world. And, most of all, I want to partner with my Wise Inner Counselor to complete the great work that is mine to do.

In fact, *Reflections on Doing Your Great Work in Any Occupation* is the title of the companion book to this volume—for being and doing are really two halves of the same process that our True Self fashions throughout our lives.

These books are reflective of the evolution of my own perception of what it means to be your True Self and to engage that Self as Love in action. These books are written for those of you whose greatest desire is to transcend your former self, because that is exactly what the Wise Inner Counselor does.

With transformation in mind and with the understanding that our reach must exceed our grasp in this life, it is my hope that you will find the reflections in this book and its partner useful on your own path of Self-discovery.

May your Wise Inner Counselor guide and guard you all the days of your life.

Cheryl Lafferty Eckl
Spring 2021

Contents

Part Four ~ Being True to Your Self

Part Five ~ Oneness in the Light of Your Wise Inner Counselor

A Bit of This and That

*If you had any idea
of who and what you really are,
you would not doubt.*

*You would run
to greet that Self at dawn,
rejoicing in each new day
of creative opportunity.*

*When such feelings begin at home,
the entire world is blessed.*

—*The Wise Inner Counselor*™

PART ONE

Who Is This Wise Inner Counselor?

YOUR BEST FRIEND IS WITHIN YOU

Move forward into the presence of your
True Self. See it. Feel it. Accept it.
Love it, and it will only increase.

The One Who Points the Way

Have you ever longed for a best friend who knows all your secrets and loves you anyway?

Someone who holds you in sincere affection and always tells you the truth because that is their nature?

Someone who perceives who you really are and persistently urges you to be more genuine, more loving, more accomplished today than you were yesterday?

Someone who steadfastly points the way to your highest potential with unfailing accuracy, and offers creative solutions that are uniquely applicable to you?

Such a friend already exists—within you.

A Great Mystery of Being

It may be hard to imagine that such a presence actually lives within each of us, but that is one of the great mysteries of being that poets, philosophers, theologians and saints have pondered since the beginning of time.

Fortunately, when we listen very carefully, in those moments when we allow the busyness of daily life to recede, we can experience a profound sense that we possess an inner voice of wisdom that already knows how to skillfully navigate a world dizzied by the accelerating pace of ever-changing events.

Nearly every conceptual system has coined a term for this inner guide. Some cultural traditions call it the still small voice, although for many it is a voice of power.

Others prefer intuition—the ability to gain direct knowledge through a higher, more refined mind which operates independently of human reasoning. Many people refer to the inner voice as their conscience, an internal compass that points them toward positive thought and action.

I call this presence the True Self or Wise Inner Counselor. Over the years I have come to know this Self as a fount of limitless inspiration and the source of my attunement with unseen elements of life.

Whatever we call the inner voice, when we pay attention to its promptings by showing up for life as we are inspired, it can act as the perfect guardian of our destiny. And it always speaks for a higher Love that improves the lives of everyone it touches.

Speaking into the Spaces

One possible reason for the mystery of inner guidance is that its voice can only be heard when we create openings through which it can reach us.

If our minds are crammed with thoughts, our emotions spinning in turmoil, our bodies occupied in constant motion, our ears filled with noise, the voice of inner wisdom quite literally cannot get a word in edgewise.

For me, getting better acquainted with my True Self has meant building quiet time into my day. I have discovered the importance of adding more "being" spaces in the midst of all my doing.

Those spaces need not be long, but they do need to be based on an open heart and mind—just in case that voice of inner wisdom has something to whisper into the secret place where my best friend lives within me.

Who Is Listening?

If the Wise Inner Counselor is speaking, what part of me is listening? I am quite certain the receptive aspect of my being is not my outer self, because flashes of inner guidance seem to bypass human thought.

As I sit with this question of who or what is receptive, I recognize the receiver as my soul—that tender part of me who has been burdened by the world's unreality and who longs for a purer, simpler life that will elevate my day-to-day existence.

When I listen to the voice of my True Self with both my inner and outer ears, my soul feels assured that the way to that uplifting life is as close as my heartbeat.

How Does Insight Come to Us?

I am fascinated by how inner guidance appears in the lives of other people. When the opportunity arises, I like to ask them, "Where or when do you get your best ideas?" Invariably, they will say things like:

- In the shower.
- First thing in the morning or late at night.
- Driving a familiar route.
- Going for a walk or run.
- Doing housework or mowing the lawn.

One of my favorite responses is, "When I have been wrestling with a problem and I finally give up trying to solve it."

Personally, I have learned never to leave the house without a notebook and pen. Without fail, the next piece of whatever writing project I am working on will come sailing in to my awareness and I have to quickly write it down before I forget what I heard.

The message may be something as simple as which route to take when I am driving. Or when to take care of a certain task. Or when *not* to do something I was planning. Or when to avoid a certain person or situation.

Those flashes of guidance that come as warnings are often the most important.

Reflection 2

REASONS FOR LISTENING

*Sometimes promptings from the Wise Inner
Counselor are life-saving interventions.*

Heeding a Serious Warning

In my late twenties I became convinced that life went along more smoothly if I paid attention to the promptings of my Wise Inner Counselor and then followed its advice.

I had occasion to prove the truth of that belief when I joined a theater troupe that moved from Denver, Colorado, to San Francisco, California, to produce an original musical written by the group's director. The show was well-received, but it did not run long enough to support any of us financially.

Our director had connections in Nebraska, so we all moved to Omaha and mounted a nightclub revue with material from Broadway musicals and classic numbers from the American songbook.

Again, the show closed before it made any money, leaving me too broke to return to the Bay Area, where I still had an apartment. So I stayed with a friend in Denver and worked for several weeks at my old waitress job until I earned enough cash to get home.

I was preparing to drive back to San Francisco when I had a sudden premonition that I was going to die in a car accident out in the middle of Nevada. I took this warning very seriously and postponed my departure, not sure what to do.

Following the Promptings

While delaying my trip, I felt a strong prompting to go see some friends perform at a local dinner theater. I knew they had found a spiritual teaching which they really liked, so after the show I mentioned my trepidation to them.

In turn, they told me about the protection they had found in giving prayers and mantras to Archangel Michael and other beings of great spiritual power. This material felt like a very timely addition to my practice of listening for inner guidance.

The next morning my friends armed me with a book of prayers, I packed up my car and set off for California—faithfully reciting the mantras to Archangel Michael and listening for more inner guidance. I visualized spiritual protection all around me and made it safely back to San Francisco.

However, on a lonely stretch of highway out in the barren wastelands of Nevada, I happened to look in the rear-view mirror. In that moment a very strong impression came to me that I had passed through the spot where the accident in my premonition would have taken place, had I not listened to the Wise Inner Counselor's prompting to visit my friends.

Learning to Trust Inner Guidance When It Matters Most

We often do not know what inspiration from inner guidance is meant to accomplish until much later. Still, following the direction of our Wise Inner Counselor when it makes little logical sense may become our most valuable daily practice—a lesson I learned from my husband, Stephen, who conscientiously followed that lead.

Around the same time that my career as a management course instructor was taking off, Stephen was diagnosed with terminal colon cancer. As his illness worsened over the ensuing four-plus years, circumstances made it imperative for each of us to rely more consciously on the guidance of our personal Wise Inner Counselor.

While Stephen focused on dealing with the burdens of cancer and its treatment, I tried hard to understand why life was pulling me in paradoxical directions.

Why was I being called out into the world as an instructor, when my greatest desire was to stay home and spend every possible hour with the love of my life, who was going to leave me all too soon? The answer eventually came in the course of unfolding events.

Opening to "Just Knowing"

Only in the final months of Stephen's life did I realize the ability to "just know" what my Wise Inner Counselor was trying to convey to me in the business classroom was exactly the skill I would need in order to care for my husband as our time together slipped away.

Students were often amazed when I would answer a question they were preparing to ask. Or when I would notice that something was puzzling them. Or when I would simply say what members of the class were thinking about a particular topic.

To them it seemed magical. To me, that ability to be surprisingly appropriate came from the trust I was developing in my Wise Inner Counselor. When I heard something, I said something—even if it made little sense at the time. The positive feedback from many students nearly always explained what the inner voice had meant.

The Caregiver's Test of Attunement

Stephen's absolute reliance on his Wise Inner Counselor was my inspiration to hold tight to my own inner guidance, especially in the last few weeks of his life when I was his sole caregiver.

Dying is the most intimate experience any of us will ever have. Stephen was a very private person who preferred to go through the process of leaving this world with as little interference as possible. And yet, as his strength waned, he needed more of my care, not less.

My challenge was to be highly attuned to his needs so I could be available to him without being emotionally intrusive. I also had to pay attention to my own well-being so I didn't fall apart when he needed me the most.

Inner guidance was the key. The situation could not be figured out logically. There was no logic to our daily experience. We simply had to be in it. Looking back on the events that transpired and some of the amazing insights we shared in Stephen's last days, I believe that the True Self of each of us united to show us the way.

By following the "knowing" sense of the Wise Inner Counselor, both Stephen and I were able to be at peace and express our deepest love and appreciation for each other throughout the most trying moments of his illness and death.

Our last Christmas together with our puppy, Bentley.

Reflection 3

As Close as Your Heartbeat

*In great ways and small, the Wise Inner Counselor
urges you to the oneness that is its essence.*

Guidance Is Right Here

In all our doing, the Wise Inner Counselor urges us to listen, listen, listen. This loving presence is only a breath away, as it conveyed to me one day in meditation.

> *Flow with the stream of life. Soar with the wind. Bask in the warm glow of Love that enlivens your soul. Breathe in the fragrance of my presence. Here in this communion we are one. Embrace the guidance you seek in this moment and you will know where and when and how to be.*

Always Appropriate

I have come to experience my Wise Inner Counselor as a connecting force that weaves my spirituality and my humanity in an unfolding spiral of inspiration, insight and compassion.

It holds no sense of limitation or judgment and many times over has created life-changing breakthroughs when I have accepted its guidance.

My Wise Inner Counselor is perfectly attuned to present circumstances. Its direction is always appropriate to the moment, whether it is prompting me, warning me or illumining my life in everyday challenges as well as through major transitions.

While not a flatterer, it does steadfastly champion my unique reason for being. It understands my hopes, dreams and longings. And it opens the way for me to make a difference in this world by bringing its presence to life.

Seeking a New Stage of Development

Learning to partner with the True Self can be profoundly illumining, even exalting. That process can also precipitate dramatic changes in our way of being. A new life goal may emerge.

We may find ourselves desiring to refine our everyday consciousness so that we may turn the temporary experience of extraordinary oneness with our True Self into a permanent stage of development.

This is possible because the Wise Inner Counselor is always urging us to reach higher, deeper and wider in all matters pertaining to our well-being.

When we accept the applicability of its guidance in our daily affairs, we can build a momentum of inner connection that accelerates our learning and soul growth in every aspect of life.

A Quality of Being

Our Wise Inner Counselor is the spirit of being behind all of our most worthy doing. It is the quality of heart that inspires us to aim for the stars at work and at home.

It is that ineffable "something" that shines through our best efforts and ignites those sublime *a-ha!* moments of creativity and innovation when a golden idea sails in, seemingly from nowhere.

When life gets tough, the Wise Inner Counselor may arrive as a miraculous ability to redeem our failures or losses, transforming our worst experiences into our most important life lessons.

I find it comforting that the Wise Inner Counselor is equally concerned with the material as well as the spiritual. It contains no separation, no duality, no opposites or paradoxes.

Rather, it offers unity and the brisk wind of Spirit that can elevate all our perceptions. In the balance of its sublime presence, great work emerges, scenting life with the fragrance of a soul's uniqueness, glistening with the radiance of a job well done in any part of life.

With the True Self at work, all our endeavors can be joyful in their completion.[1]

Always Available, Always in Motion

Our True Self is neither subject to nor dependent upon the approval of others. It requires only our loving attention and commitment to bring our best efforts to life.

The Wise Inner Counselor thrives in our positive self-regard. And its voice grows stronger in our willingness to receive the guidance it unfailingly beams to us throughout our life.

This deeply personal conversation between inspiration and practical application is the Wise Inner Counselor's daily gift for resolving our hour-by-hour experience of being and doing. For doing and being are twin aspects of our life—apparently separate, yet ultimately unified as we embody Love in action.

Being in the Realm of Choice

We place a great deal of attention on the physical aspects of life because that is what we can see. And, indeed, the physical is where we determine how much of the spiritual can act in our lives.

The material world is the realm of choice. Will we choose to infuse our thoughts, words and deeds with the energy of the Wise Inner Counselor who is completely dedicated to our highest purpose? Or will we decide to "go it alone" as a law unto ourselves?

Free will reigns supreme in our universe. We can choose not to engage the loving presence of our True Self. But that would be a bit like knowing there is a treasure buried in our back yard and deciding that getting out a shovel to dig is too much trouble.

Be That Oneness

Do you hear the voice of Love? Do you feel the sublime presence of a universe waiting to share the blessing of your attention?

Harmony is the domain of inner wisdom. Would you increase the volume of its messages?

Seek peace. Be at peace. Seek oneness. Be that oneness.

Reflection 4

ENGAGING IN THE HIGHEST GOOD

*The highest good is universal as well as
personal, and the True Self embodies both.*

Seeking the Best for All

Achieving the most positive results for an individual or group can
have far-reaching benefits—like the proverbial vibration caused by
the flapping of a butterfly's wing which can ripple around the planet
to effect change in far-distant places.

Ideally, those changes will prove beneficial to all concerned.
Regardless of the situation, your True Self carefully weighs current
circumstances, calculates the best possible outcome and inspires
you to take appropriate action to achieve that outcome.

Your Wise Inner Counselor Is All About Connection

This essence of who we really are is profoundly personal. When we
engage with our Wise Inner Counselor, we are connected to all that
is good and true and beautiful about us—in our own unique way.

The more we allow that presence to act in our world, the
more we will naturally engage in the highest good for ourselves and
others. The process is just that simple and it is exactly that hard.

Being deeply committed to the highest good is:

Aspirational: We desire it with our whole heart.

Inspirational: The messages from our True Self are uplifting and motivating.

Perspirational: We accept that giving our Wise Inner Counselor our full attention takes work.

Transformational: We soon realize that the presence of Love will not leave us unchanged.

Engagement's Texture

Bonding with inner guidance can be a bit like a contact sport. Until we experience a tangible, or what some call a "felt sense" of connection, we probably are not fully engaged with our True Self.

However, when we are plugged in to that presence, we may feel a resonance, almost an electrical charge, that tingles through our body, mind and soul. Novel ideas may pop into our awareness to spark a new creation or solve a problem.

We may feel an exceptional warmth in our heart. Perhaps an inner light that radiates in or around us. Or we may notice a certain confidence or maturity that is absent when we are worried or in the throes of an unhealthy psychological pattern.

Unexpected Waves of Joy

One startling confirmation that we and our Wise Inner Counselor are fully engaged in a partnership may be when waves of joy come wafting in for no apparent reason.

These moments of unexpected elation are some of life's most sublime. They open the heart—delighting the senses and permeating the environment with enthusiasm and a feeling of hope.

This joy is comforting, reassuring—like a firm hug and a soft hand laid upon our brow, soothing away all worry and concern that we may not be up to the challenges before us.

Musing About the True Self

As a way of connecting with my Wise Inner Counselor, I often let my awareness rest quietly with the intention of inviting this inner presence to teach me about itself.

Here are some of those musings:

The Wise Inner Counselor is like a precious gem—possessed of many facets, yet simple in its wholeness.

The diamond-shining being of our True Self is polished in the heat and pressure of life.

Like the force that transforms a lump of coal into a glistening diamond, life presses us to align with the unique inner pattern that is the emblem of our reality.

In this process we are becoming congruent with the inner structure of the priceless jewel that is the True Self.

The True Self is lit from within with a brilliance all its own. We are uniquely individual in how our inner light flashes and beams into the world.

Whether at work or at home, we are lovingly challenged to be more reliable, more kind, wise and powerful in our expression of the truth, beauty and goodness that emanate from our Wise Inner Counselor's presence.

The Wise Inner Counselor Transforms as It Goes

The more we grow in our ability to collaborate with our True Self, we may become aware that our life is changing in character and quality.

At least that has been my personal experience.

I see the Wise Inner Counselor operating like an alchemist, refining the lead of a world's chaotic complexity into the gold of heightened awareness of inner patterns or what one of my favorite poets, William Wordsworth, called "the life of things."

In his exquisite poem, *Tintern Abbey*, he wrote that it is "with an eye made quiet by the power of harmony, and the deep power of joy" that we perceive the essence of life. And with that perception, myriad facets of the True Self flash and sparkle.

From his meditations on the natural order of his English homeland's countryside, Wordsworth came to understand a fundamental truth: Out of the patterns of inner guidance what is most important emerges as:

> ...that best portion of a good man's life;
> His little, nameless, unremembered acts
> Of kindness and of love.[2]

Seeking Simple Settings

It is so easy to make a tangle of life and work. If we spend inordinate amounts of time in complexity, we may lose sight of the power of harmony that can create lasting value in our lives.

When we focus on the mere acquisition of information or material possessions, our minds and hearts, homes and offices can get cluttered with the dross of useless cleverness that blocks the inner voice.

Thinking again of that priceless jewel of Self, the Wise Inner Counselor says it this way:

> *The simplest settings allow the greatest light*
> *to shine through life.*

Grounded in Reality

The Wise Inner Counselor accesses ways of knowing which our human minds do not. It sees the past, present and future as a unity while perfectly directing us moment by moment in response to changing circumstances.

The more attuned we are to this timeless flow of guidance, the more trustworthy we become. And the more able we are to respond with love, wisdom and the appropriate amount of energy in any given situation.

Our True Self is practical because it is actual, not theoretical. Inner knowing is not magic—although it may seem so in those flashes of insight that transcend mental struggle and synthesize myriad details into an elegant, holistic solution.

We soar to Wisdom's heights because we are gifted with a firm foundation in the realities of inner guidance, which also enhances skills we may gain through expert training, depth of experience and focused knowledge.

Speaking for the Presence of Love

The goal in bringing inner guidance to the forefront of life is to focus on the convergence of our spirituality and our humanity where they meet in sublime communion in the heart.

For me, that focus has meant coming to know my Wise Inner Counselor as the inner presence which has the ability to communicate with refined realms of Love and also with my soul.

I realize that my soul, as the most vulnerable aspect of my being, has lost contact with higher levels of consciousness and so requires a mediator—a translator of sorts—who can bridge the gap between worlds.

This is true for each of us, and is the primary function of the Wise Inner Counselor. It communes with Love and then transmits that spiritual essence to us in flashes of insight, peak experiences and transcendent events that raise our human consciousness out of the ego state of the false self.

In this way, the True Self transcends that false self, rendering it irrelevant so that outworn, habitual patterns of behavior, thought and feeling fall away, dissolving into the infinite Love that is both the source and goal of all life.

Reflection 5

A Life Lived to the Full

*One person who outpictures their True Self can
make a huge difference in the lives of others.*

Looking to Our Role Models

When we are very young we look to our parents, other primary
caregivers or perhaps a special teacher as the embodiment of the
Wise Inner Counselor. As we mature, we gradually learn that the
true guidance which will carry us through life comes from within.

However, before we grow into that realization, we rely upon
those role models closest to us. The quality of that experience
shapes the subsequent development of our personal psychology
and informs our relationship with every other individual whom we
encounter.

Common-Sense Parents

I was extremely fortunate to have two parents who were teachers at
heart and by profession, and who lived their lives with the common
sense they had gleaned from their own upbringing in a rural community in the Missouri Ozarks.

In thinking about my father in particular, I can see that I grew
up in the presence of a parent who was very integrated with his

Wise Inner Counselor. Of course, he wasn't perfect. But my father was a man of impeccable character. One sensed that about him.

Looking back on my childhood, I can feel that I absorbed much of what I try to emulate in my own life from the example that he set, especially during those times when I was hanging out with him in his workshop as he repaired radios and televisions or when he was helping me with my math homework.

An Early Awakening

My father was a quiet man who did not talk about himself. He let his deeds and the humor that would often come out in his dry wit convey who and what he was.

It was not until he received what turned out to be a false positive cancer diagnosis that he and I had a heart-to-heart talk about life and death as it was about to dramatically affect us. He wanted to know if I was happy in my marriage (I was), and I wanted to know if he was right with his God (he was).

"Let's go to the bowling alley diner. We can talk there," he said one morning soon after Stephen and I had driven through a spring snowstorm between Montana and Arizona to be with my parents as they faced my father's potentially life-threatening diagnosis.

I grabbed my jacket and sat quietly in the car as my father drove to the diner, only ten minutes away. Then, over cups of weak coffee, we told each other the truth about our lives. I do not remember what I said, but my father's story is etched in my memory.

He told me that as a young man recently graduated from high school and contemplating his future, he attended a Chautauqua revival meeting—one of those "old time religion" events that were held in a big tent where a minister would preach the Gospel.

When it came time for the altar call, my father went forward with others who had been inspired by the sermon. He said that as he knelt there, a comforting warmth came over his whole body.

In that moment, he felt himself being assured that "everything would always be alright" in his life.

"And you know, it always has been," he affirmed with a smile and an upward gaze that spoke volumes about the inner guidance that had been his True North since that transformational event.

Essence of a Developed Heart

We each outpicture the connection with our Wise Inner Counselor differently. And yet I believe there are several major characteristics of the developed heart that shine out from the True Self.

Integrity

To me, integrity means an integration between one's words and deeds. My father was like that. He was unabashedly himself. There appeared to be no separation between his inner and outer worlds.

He had firm principles and he lived by them with a quiet dignity which people (including his young daughter) respected.

He definitely had his opinions, but I do not remember him ever treating anyone with anything other than the same respect he afforded to every other person—whether they were the minister at our church or the waitress who served the Friday night chicken dinners our family enjoyed at our favorite restaurant.

Wisdom

Wisdom comes from experience and reflection on the essence of things. My father's take on life was neither random nor rushed. He did not jump to conclusions. Instead, he considered many options and then decided. I now see that inner guidance played a large part in the wisdom he did his best to convey to me.

I remember that if he disagreed with me, I never felt attacked. He just disagreed with my point of view and usually found a way to help me make a more effective decision.

Intellect often accompanies wisdom, and my father's was impressive. He began his electronics career by building crystal radios as a boy. When I was a child he taught electronics for the Air Force and eventually retired as a technical training instructor on the space shuttle program.

My mother told the story of someone asking my father how cells phones worked. This was years before everyone owned their own device. His answer was to the point. "I've not studied them, but I can tell you how they should work." And then he went on to describe exactly how cells phones actually do work.

Will Power

One did not have to be around my father for long to sense the strength of his will power. He persevered through many difficult circumstances to live the life of integrity from which I do not believe he ever wavered.

Whether he was standing up to government contractors who were trying to ship defective electronics during World War II or figuring out the best way to teach the course on space shuttle logistics he was writing, he had the courage of his convictions and the will to see them through.

Love

Do we as children ever really understand how much our caregivers love us? I know I did not realize the depth of my father's affection until I was getting married to Stephen. I was talking to my mother about plans and expenses and she said, "You know your father will give you anything you want."

Until that moment, I did not realize how constantly my father had looked out for me and how devoted he was to my happiness. From that day forward I tried to never take his love for granted.

Joy

You cannot fake joy. My father exuded a genuine cheerfulness that I remember seeing in him when he was working in his strawberry patch or when we were fishing or when he was building something in his workshop.

I think the joy he brought to life was also a result of having looked death in the face in a way that probably is common to those who have grown up in the country surrounded by a large extended family. Loss is a constant companion when you live with Nature's life and death cycles in the raising of crops and animals, and in the company of elderly relatives who reach the end of their lives and pass away from any number of causes.

Into the Arms of Love

My own life has shown me that when we know in our heart of hearts that not even death can separate us from our true identity, nothing has the power to derail us from embracing a life that expresses the essential qualities of the Wise Inner Counselor.

The day before my father died, my mother was speaking to him about their fifty-seven years of married life. She said to him, "We'll just remember the good times, not the things that went wrong." My father looked at her and said in all sincerity, "Did anything go wrong?"

That is the perspective of someone who is transiting out of this world through the heart of his Wise Inner Counselor into the arms of Love. Not long after that conversation, my father slipped into a coma and passed away a few hours later with a serene smile on his lips.

When the Inspiring Ones Depart

When such people as my father depart, they leave a gaping hole in the lives of those who were blessed to know them. Their absence affects us in ways we could not have anticipated until they are gone.

Now we realize that we must fill the very large shoes of one who stood head and shoulders above the rest of us, even when he was only five feet, six inches tall.

The sudden absence of this loved one can become a call to action for those of us who remain. We are suddenly inspired to develop our own impeccability and transcend what we may now observe as petty, lukewarm ways of being.

We find ourselves aspiring to do more, to be better today than we were yesterday. To reach out to our fellow creatures and work together for decency and principles, not the ideologies and isms that blind many to the actual effects of their actions.

When someone can encourage us to follow in their footsteps that were walked in the light of inner guidance, truly, that is a life well lived.

My father in his home office with his poster of the space shuttle he worked on holding pride of place.

PART TWO

On Life's Journey with Your

Wise Inner Counselor™

INCREASING THE VOLUME OF INNER GUIDANCE

*One challenge in listening for the voice
of the Wise Inner Counselor is that
we are often too busy to hear it.*

Paying Closer Attention

The subtle voice of inner guidance is easy to ignore, override or argue with until we decide to pay more consistent attention to its promptings.

Even after a lifetime of listening, I still find myself resisting the guidance of my Wise Inner Counselor when it points me toward a particularly difficult task. Still more challenging is following inner wisdom when I must let go of long-held perspectives about my way of being in the world.

Letting Go of Control

I have always been a "make it happen" kind of person. So accepting that I am not in charge of my life's progress is a big shift which I am called upon to make every day and which I advocate for others.

Oh, that following my own advice were so easy! I am always happy to start a new project—and I am even more satisfied when that project is completed. Starting and finishing require a lot of thinking and planning. The key for me is to keep all that mental activity in balance.

As soon as I find myself believing that I have a project nicely figured out, I know it is time to stop hurtling toward the finish line and take a long, hard look at what I am actually doing. A course correction from my Wise Inner Counselor is usually on the horizon.

Listening as a Spiritual Practice

For years I assumed I did not have a spiritual practice because I have never been inclined to long sessions of seated contemplation. Instead, I create an environment of outer peace and quiet. Then I listen and write what I hear.

Of course, this is a spiritual practice. Listening connects me with my inner wisdom, and I have followed this habit for so long that it is now a way of being. Inspiration comes to me most often when my thinking brain is receptive.

Hospitality Awakens the Wise Inner Counselor

My mother often spoke of "entertaining angels unawares." To her that meant extending a welcoming spirit toward new people as well as to her friends and family.

Her innate hospitality created space in her life for others and for her own inner guidance—which she followed with admirable grace. She had an uncanny sense of timing about all sorts of things.

I have found this same gracious openness in my travels to the Emerald Isle, where hospitality is legendary. In the West of Ireland, where I have visited several times, the legend is true.

Whether on a formal tour or spending a day of solo exploring in a quaint Irish village, I have found the people to be welcoming and amazingly attuned to their own Wise Inner Counselor.

Some of those I am privileged to know as friends seem to live in the flow of inner guidance. Because they are hospitable to inspiration, they are equally open to their fellow creatures. And even when discussing life's end (you cannot be in the West of Ireland for long without the subject of death arising), they are joyful in their appreciation of life in all of its convoluted variableness.

Going Out of Sync

One reason that the Wise Inner Counselor often emerges in times of crisis is that loss of any kind throws us out of sync with our normal way of being in the world.

This "twilight zone" state of consciousness that is neither here nor there is a familiar habitation of inner guidance. It is also a highly creative space that artists know very well.

Years ago when I was teaching a course on creative problem solving, I learned about a brain wave called "Theta" that corresponds to this state. Those coveted *Eureka!* moments that come sailing in as shimmering orbs of inspiration demonstrate this wave length.

Successful inventors like Thomas Edison, who reportedly took power naps in his roll-top desk,[3] learn how to increase the occurrence of the Theta state. We can do the same by observing when we get our best ideas. When we do more of whatever that is, the voice of inner guidance will likely get clearer.

Honoring the Contact

The Wise Inner Counselor attends us and lives within us. It is not separate from us unless we choose to turn away.

Of course, we have free will, but our inner guidance will always be there, speaking wisely, illuminating the right path, guarding our footsteps, lest we fall away from that path.

The volume of the communication depends on us.

William Blake said it best: "He knows himself greatly who never opposes his genius." That genius is the essence of our Wise Inner Counselor.

Be a Friend to Your Wise Inner Counselor

We might consider our relationship with our deepest human friend-ships and the faithful love we share. I believe that our relationship with our Wise Inner Counselor can be even more enduring.

When we are friends with someone:

We look forward to spending time together.

We are kind to one another and provide each other with appropriate help in times of need.

We share many common interests, not the least of which is one another's well-being.

We give each other gifts, and we cherish those gifts because we know they were given in recognition of our interests and in sup-port of our finest qualities.

We also pay attention to the suggestions our best friends offer, which is another type of gift.

When they warn us about some impending danger, we heed that warning and take appropriate action.

Invoking More Positive Energy into Our Lives

The True Self lives in the realm of higher consciousness. When we invoke spiritual energy through prayer, meditation and especially through chants, mantras and devotional songs, we are clearing the way for improved communication.

The process is rather like increasing the bandwidth from an Internet Service Provider, upgrading a cell phone or acquiring a more sensitive tuner for a radio.

What we are trying to do is clear our internal channels for better reception of the higher frequencies of inner guidance. When we do that, our thoughts, words and deeds are more in alignment with our Wise Inner Counselor, making its voice louder.

Taking Action

To me, working with inner guidance is a bit like exercising a muscle.

The more I engage it, the stronger it grows. When anyone asks me for the surest way to increase the volume of inner wisdom, here is what I tell them:

Move forward with genuine anticipation into the presence of your Wise Inner Counselor. See it, feel it, accept it. Use it and it will only increase. The result of your communion can fill you with exquisite peace and joy.

Reflection 7

CORE VALUES REFLECT YOUR TRUE SELF

*Core values are the very essence
of the Wise Inner Counselor.*

Positive Inner Motivators

Those unseen, though powerfully felt, positive internal motivators called core values come to us from the Wise Inner Counselor. Their tangible presence affirms that we are acting on behalf of the highest good for everyone involved in the circumstances of our life and work.

That "good" is the Wise Inner Counselor's unwavering attention which gives us the courage to risk all for the sake of another and the willingness to be vulnerable and ask for help when we need it.

As Vital as the Air We Breathe

Without core values, we are rudderless wanderers in a vast unknown sea of life. These foundational motivating principles are the pearl of great price that we willingly give our last breath to defend.

We will leave companies, marriages, families or nations when our values are so violated as to make our continued presence there untenable. While we may observe core values beaming through

familiar mental constructs, they really exist outside of those structures. Values may inform our beliefs, yet they do not operate at the
cognitive level where beliefs hold sway.

Core values are not even faith. Rather, they flow from the very
essence of our True Self, reflecting our innermost identity.

Following Guiding Principles

Core values shine out as beacons from an inner lighthouse of
being that we each possess. Core values are the barometer by
which we measure the quality of our life and our work. We define
our personal integrity by these guiding principles. They form the
basis of both individual and organizational missions and visions.

One way to evaluate if you are operating in sync with your
Wise Inner Counselor is to ask yourself if your attitudes, behaviors
and competencies align with your core values. When you look in the
mirror, do you see your highest principles reflecting back to you?

Discovering Your Core Values

As children we absorb our family's core values as mother's milk—
thinking, feeling and behaving within that unconscious structure

until we can begin to form our own value system. Of course, the challenge is that, even as adults, we may not be consciously aware of what we value most in life and work.

Core values are as unique as a fingerprint and often as illusive as a butterfly on the wing. In trying to articulate your guiding principles, it can be helpful to research what other individuals and organizations have identified as their core values.

Sometimes reviewing a list of possible core values will spark that internal *a-ha!* when a particular word resonates. Engaging in a discussion with others about core values can be an enlightening experience. It can also be rather frustrating.

Some Values Are Best Kept Personal

A co-worker told the story of working with a team on the value of freedom. Going into the discussion this congenial group assumed they all agreed on what freedom meant. However, as the conversation developed, growing more heated as disagreements arose, the group finally decided that freedom was far too individual a concept to adopt as a shared core value.

I always encourage my workshop participants to consider what they value most because of the potentially rich experience that awaits their deep exploration of the guiding principles that inspire and motivate them every day.

To discover the true meaning of my own core values, I had to expand my gaze, open my heart and listen very attentively to the voice of my Wise Inner Counselor. When I allowed myself that deeper, wider exploration, amazing insights flooded into my awareness and actually changed elements of my self-perception.

Only You Can Identify Your Core Values

Other people are likely to assume they know your core values based on your affiliation or lack of affiliation with certain groups. You may even choose to join a group or go to work for a particular company because you share core values—and that is a very good place to start.

However, until you experience a solid communion with the guiding principles you select, you will be missing an opportunity to discover who you are in the very heart of your being. You cannot really claim a value as core until you follow it all the way to the depths of its meaning—which may not be immediately apparent.

Your True Self has a frequency, an electronic charge that resonates like a note on a musical scale. Your infant ears, or perhaps your mother's, may have heard that ethereal tone sounded at your birth.

I am told that some modern mothers have revived an indigenous tradition of going out alone into Nature's silence so they may hear the song of their newborn's soul. As the baby grows, the mother sings the soul-song to help her child stay connected to his or her destiny.

Obviously, this practice requires profound attunement with the baby's identity before and after birth so that what emerges is the child's song rather than the mother's interpretation. Mothers who access this insightful communion reward their children and themselves with an intimacy that can last a lifetime.

Flooded with the Joy of Self-Discovery

Your essential core values vibrate with the tone of your True Self. Outer techniques will not reveal their reality to you. Only deep attunement will allow your heart to detect the subtle resonance between your unique frequency and the principles that flow from it.

I can tell you from my own communion with guiding principles that the experience of touching into my most essential core value was unlike any self-help or personal growth technique I had explored over the previous several decades.

This value seemed to possess an essence behind it as a personified force that brought the principle to life. When I contacted that essence in my Wise Inner Counselor, the sensation was almost as if I had been created from that spirit.

I knew I was home. Something in me landed and I suddenly saw dozens of clues to my true identity that had been right in front of me for years.

It didn't matter that others said, "Oh, yes, I always knew that about you." Until I did some concentrated inner exploration, I did not know—and that is the point.

"The Poetess" original artwork by David Moore.
Commissioned by the author.

Reflection 8

THE WONDER OF WISDOM

Sometimes to understand a core value, we must
look away from where we think we will find it.

Starting Fresh

We approach a core value with beginner's mind—without preconceptions or notions of what we think we know. For then, and only then, will the spirit of that value be free to speak to us of its true nature, which may also be ours.

I had that experience while contemplating Wisdom as a personal core value. I would like to share with you what I discovered.

What Is Wisdom?

I had always thought of Wisdom as a quality of mind. To be sure, it is a quality of the higher mind of the True Self. Yet when I searched for Wisdom in my own head, I did not find it.

When I sought it in my heart, I discovered Wisdom at home, curled up by the fire, glowing with a radiance that transforms all unlike itself, illuminating the best way forward in any given moment.

Wisdom's Texture

Wisdom's insight may arrive quietly or like a thunderbolt, and its effect is never fleeting. It stays with us and in us, working a subtle magic that is as transformative as it is informative.

Willing to Appear Foolish

To be wise is the mind's most glorious capability, yet the mind alone cannot achieve it. Only when endowed with the willingness to be thought a fool is the mind able to be truly wise.

Shakespeare understood this concept well and wrote the Fool in *King Lear* as the only wise person in the play. The Fool was not afraid to tell the truth and he knew when to tell it.

He understood the foolishness of those who lusted for power, and the vulnerability of those like Lear and his daughter Cordelia who did not understand the wily nature of the ego mind.

Wisdom's Challenge

Why is Wisdom so difficult to perceive? Is it because it flies in the face of our defenses, our masks and the ego's arrogance that convinces us that knowledge of facts and figures alone will guarantee success in life and work?

In aspiring to be clever, do we push Wisdom away?

In grasping after more information, do we cloud the inner knowing that would tell us where and how to be?

In turning up the volume of distractions, do we drown out the bright voice of Wisdom that is also loving and strong?

Wisdom Is Dynamic

Wisdom is not an outer goal to be pursued, a certificate to be earned or a degree plaque to hang on the wall.

It comes to the receptive heart and the humble mind that yearn to understand the Universe's mysteries. Not to control or manipulate them, but to plumb their depths. To partner with them as co-creators in a world in desperate need of illumination.

Facts act like static elements until enlivened by Wisdom's

dynamic life force that connects the dots of our learning, embellishing some aspects and eliminating others.

We may know all things, but without a heart in which to place data in context, we are likely to miss the Wisdom boat that sails all the way to joy.

Wisdom's Intention

Wisdom's deeper purpose is to trigger change, to shake up patterns of thinking and feeling that have overstayed their usefulness in our work and life. And to replace them with the freshness of all that is innately unique to the soul.

For Wisdom's intention is clarity of mind and purity of heart, operating like a sandblaster stripping away centuries of grime to reveal a glistening cathedral underneath.

In this case, our soul is the edifice whose joyful reality Wisdom uncovers—overcoming self-condemnation and any sense of worthlessness that might hold us back from our destiny.

Wisdom does not judge or shame or blame or condemn. It simply discerns, dividing our erroneous concepts of identity (and we all have them) from the reality of our True Self.

The Wise Inner Counselor puts it this way:

You are so much more than you realize. Look beyond roles and titles, status and labels. Look to your heart and find there the Wisdom you have internalized in this life through hard-won experience and inner knowing. In your heart is the reward for right action and the source of all right decisions. We call it joy.

Harmony Is Key

We do not so much gain Wisdom as attract it. The Wise Inner Counselor is drawn to a peaceful presence and then enhances it—moving with the breath, calming the mind, stilling the nerves, easing the heart's burdens.

We are only as wise as our bodies and minds are relaxed and our hearts open to the present moment. Otherwise, tension blocks Wisdom like an electrical short in our internal wiring.

When body, heart and mind are at peace in one harmonious accord, we are able to retain the love and illumination we have gained. Then we may be wise.

Coming Back Around

Like the salmon that returns to its place of origin to spawn, Wisdom urges us to come full circle in life.

To complete what we have begun.

To rise up to the next turn in life's cycles.

To joyfully apply our talents and to be generous in the application of what we have accomplished so that others may live healthier, happier, more enlightened lives.

The more we learn, the more we see there is to learn. We honor the Wisdom we have absorbed through experience and study. We expect the unexpected, and we keep striving to reach further into its powerful truths.

Then we focus as much on the inner qualities of life as on our outer achievements—trusting that in the process we will be wiser and more joyful tomorrow than we are today.

Reflection 9

SAVORING WISDOM'S PRESENCE

*All the world is a schoolroom. When we are wise, we recognize
every situation as an opportunity to learn and grow.*

More to this World than Meets the Eye

We use all of our senses when we are wise. We understand the body as an excellent barometer of truth and the mind as a faithful servant that can create sturdy structures of thought and action to support our best efforts. We respect our mental capabilities, yet we do not let them dominate.

360 Senses of the Ancients

Some time ago I came across a video series called "The Pyramid Code." One of the most fascinating people interviewed was a very old man named Abd'El Hakim Awyan, who is a lineage holder in an all-but-forgotten Egyptian wisdom tradition.

He grew up within sight of the Great Pyramid and knows the area's history and geography from the inside. When he was a child, he actually went swimming in tunnels under the Sphinx complex.

Among his most astounding revelations was his statement that the ancients who built the Sphinx (many centuries earlier than is generally accepted) had access to 360 senses.

Not five or six, but 360!

I could hardly fathom what life would be like with such wisdom quite literally in one's fingertips. Yet as I sat with the concept, I became aware of the many subtle ways in which my Wise Inner Counselor transmits "knowing" to me.

When Knowing Emerges

Sometimes I will suddenly understand a conundrum I have been wrestling with, or I will gain an insight into a situation that I had not previously considered.

Often I will get a mental picture of exactly how the many tasks of my day should be accomplished. And on more than one occasion I have begun to feel uneasy about an activity that had seemed like a good idea at the time I originally planned it, but which turned out to be an unwise pursuit.

Intuition Uses all the Senses

Have you noticed your Wise Inner Counselor making use of all of your physical senses to communicate with you?

Perhaps it catches your attention through sights, sounds, textures, aromas or tastes. Or maybe you experience a flutter in your belly, a tingle up your spine or other bodily sensations.

Any one or all of these manifestations can be a sign that inner guidance has an important message for you. The more you refine your physical senses through a healthy lifestyle, the more accurately can they function as receivers of Wisdom's presence.

Built-in Cerebral Receptors

It occurs to me that one reason inner guidance can land in various places in the body is that research has shown the presence of complex neural networks in the heart and the gut that function like extensions of the brain.[4]

Considering that we know the Wise Inner Counselor has the

quality of a higher mind, it makes sense that our bodies could be endowed with receptor cells which are attuned to inner knowing.

Perhaps these faculties represent an inkling of those latent 360 senses that have atrophied in humans over centuries of being ignored.

What the Aborigines Know

In her extraordinary book, *Tracks*, adventurer Robyn Davidson tells the story of her solo trek across 1,700 miles of Australian Outback all the way to the Indian Ocean with only her dog, Diggity, and the four camels she had captured and trained for the journey.

You might appreciate the film by the same title that was produced some years ago. The cinematography really captures the extreme conditions Robyn faced. For an even better understanding of how she tapped into the kind of sensorial attunement that I think Hakim was describing, I recommend her written account.

Particularly remarkable is her description of how she learned to survive while traversing the most rugged and perilous part of her journey. She had spent several weeks being guided across sacred aboriginal land by a tribal elder, but at a certain point he was obliged to return to his village. Now she was on her own.

Robyn began to view everything around her as part of an enormous whole. She wrote:

> What was once a thing that merely existed became something that everything else acted upon and had a relationship with and vice versa. In picking up a rock, I could no longer simply say, "This is a rock." I could now say, "This is part of a net," or closer, "This, which everything acts upon, acts." [5]

I suspect this way of knowing approximates the 360 senses of the ancients. They, too, were part of the net or web of life whose boundaries between self and other were very thin in an environment that "stretched out for ever," as Robyn describes.

Given the necessary circumstances and our willingness to open our consciousness to many types of wisdom that exist beyond familiar patterns, the Wise Inner Counselor could take us there. That would be an experience to savor.

Journaling Your Way to Wisdom

Your Wise Inner Counselor has something to say to you. How will you detect that wisdom?

Wisdom Communicates in Many Ways

We all have different preferences for how we like to communicate and myriad talents for the form that communication takes.

Whether we realize it or not, we have something to say about those preferences and talents. That "something" also may be the wisdom of your Wise Inner Counselor that is falling on inattentive ears because you have not given its voice a chance to be heard.

These days there are many methods for sharing the wisdom of your True Self and the musings of your soul. Blogs in written, audio or video formats can be excellent tools. The same goes for raw art and visual journals—an appealing alternative for those of us who cannot draw, yet still appreciate the power of images.

In one way or another, each of these is a type of journal.

What Is a Journal?

The word "journal" comes from the French word "jour" meaning day. In its simplest form, a journal is the record of your day.

It can also be the starting point of your day. That is what Julia Cameron recommends in her popular work, *The Artist's Way: A Spiritual Guide to Higher Creativity.*[6] Her practice of what she calls "morning pages" has transformed many a life—my own included.

There is something about welcoming a conversation between you and your True Self over a morning cup of tea or coffee that can set the sail of your day with miraculous inspiration.

Because I tend to be a night-owl, my morning pages are often evening pages, which also can work. When I allow myself the time and space for these moments of reflection, the meaning of dramatic or seemingly insignificant events of the day come into sharper focus than I could ever accomplish by merely thinking about them or by forgetting them entirely.

Some of my most inspired writing has come from these pages. In fact, the majority of my books have emerged from these hours of unstructured, unstressed musing.

Why Does Journaling Work?

For me, journaling is useful because it allows me to objectify the thoughts, feelings and reactions to which I am subject. When I put one of these aspects of my own human condition on paper (or video or audio or in a piece of artwork), I am no longer subject to it.

It is now an object—a collection of words or sounds or visual images that I can observe, analyze, evaluate and either discard or keep. As long as those thoughts and feelings are rummaging around in my mind, often under the surface in my subconscious, they may be surreptitiously running my life. Once I can shine the light of conscious awareness on them, I am no longer their unwitting victim.

If they are positive thoughts and feelings, I would much prefer to be aware of them so I can take action to maximize their potential.

The Magic of Journaling

I am convinced that our inner voice thrives when we give it expression. Julia Cameron's exercise taught me that. When I followed her instruction to start writing—even if I had nothing original to say or was decidedly bored with my repetitive mental "churnings"—a mysterious force began to take over.

Somewhere in the middle of my scribbling, "I have nothing to say, I have nothing to say," the inner voice would declare, "I do!"

And then we were off! Pages and pages later I was writing insights about my inner world I had not been aware of. And my Wise Inner Counselor was offering possibilities, solutions and novel ideas that I had never considered.

Social Media Is Not Journaling

I believe that social media could be a wonderful mode for sharing our musings from the True Self. There is some of that in the positive quotes and beautiful images that many people post.

Unfortunately, the sad reality about much of social media is that too often the thoughts and feelings posted are the narcissistic and cruel rantings of the basest human opinions. Unless you do a lot of filtering on your social media feed, you may find yourself bombarded by negative postings from people whom you would never suspect of writing such meanness.

The voice of the Wise Inner Counselor has been all but drowned out by the ease of online snarky-ness.

A Therapeutic Process

I suggest that you keep your initial stream of consciousness private. The process of recording that stream is what counts.

When I reviewed the stack of journals I had accumulated during my husband's illness and passing, I was astounded by the repetitive worries, complaints and all-too-human thoughts I had been steadily recording. Clearly, a single journal entry did not a breakthrough make.

Thankfully, insights eventually did arise and solutions did

emerge as I let go of the thoughts and feelings that were not helpful in midst of the rough waters we were navigating.

The process was very therapeutic—which was its initial purpose. Publishing came later. The useful material I excerpted, edited and turned into a book—along with a lot of fresh writing. Once the book was published, I shredded the original journals.

Be Kind to Your Journaling Self

Not long ago I was trying to write about the concept of finding joy through engaging with the Wise Inner Counselor. However, the operative word in the previous sentence is "trying." A sure way to block the flow of inner wisdom.

I know that—and yet I was doing it anyway. So I pulled out my journal and just started writing. Here is what emerged—an example of how journaling can unlock the creativity that longs to pour out of each of us.

At the end of this unstructured flow (which became kinder as it unfolded) some lovely insights about joy emerged. I am grateful that my Wise Inner Counselor showed up because these thoughts are actually an answer to what I was "trying" to say.

A Morning's Reflections

I want to say that life begins and ends in joy, but the life circumstances of many people belie that statement.

To claim joy as a fact becomes too philosophical, too idealistic. To speak of a joyful Creator is potentially off-putting for people who are in the midst of crisis.

So how to begin?

I'm thinking too much. The only way to write of joy is to feel joy. To be in the joy of life itself. To be enfolded in the communion of unconditional ecstasy from the joy of being here. At this moment I am not there.

I must stop trying to write, to be clever, inspired, snappy, deep. Wise. Oh, definitely stop trying to be wise.

There is no wisdom in merely gritting my teeth, willing and wishing for Spirit to touch me with its otherworldly magic. Or cranking up my mental body to produce thoughts worthy of the printed page.

Trying may be worthy, but only if the motivation is love. Other "efforting" is hollow, forced, ego-based. Not reflective, but reflexive. A knee-jerk response to what calls rather than the ease of perfect synchrony.

I paused, took a breath and began again. Almost immediately, the tone changed. A different voice was speaking, offering these lovely insights.

Life begins in joy. Life births in joy. I love watching a video of a rambunctious colt racing around his mother. Or calves gamboling around a field—a bovine nursery. The drive to learn, to grow echoes across species. Like a baby ecstatic in its discovery of toes.

Be still and pay attention to life. Joy lives in the cosmic interval, the thin place between worlds.

It embodies the radiance of dawn, the glory of the setting sun—in beauty, simplicity and the elegance of uncluttered design.

Joy abounds in the thoughtful gesture and the laughter of a child. In the play of any living creature. In the green of springtime and the beauty of Love's unquenchable desire to be more Love.

Joy longs to extend itself, to multiply itself over and over in spontaneous manifestation.

Joy is one with life. Joy just *is*.

Yes, now I could feel the joy I had been trying to write about. It simply emerged from the presence of inner guidance—but only when I stopped trying.

The Importance of Letting Go

I once spoke to several people about their own experience with journaling. One woman said she was afraid a family member might discover the uncomplimentary things she had written.

My advice: Write anyway. Get those unspoken ideas on paper and then shred the lot of it. Keep a separate notebook of insights, victories and inspirations, but get rid of what neither you nor your loved ones need to encounter again.

Another woman, a middle school teacher, told me that she frequently goes back and brutally edits her journal entries, although she has never planned to publish them. I could see clearly that her self-criticism was blocking her creativity and ruining her joy.

I suggested that her initial process of giving voice to her inner world was what was important, but that condemning herself for having imperfect thoughts and feelings was self-defeating.

I proposed that she journal about what wanted to be brought into her awareness. However, instead of reviewing with an unkind eye what she had written, she could put the pages in a drawer without looking at them and then destroy them at the end of her summer break. I encouraged her to let go of the whole thing and offer herself compassion instead.

Negative thoughts and feelings will land on our heads from time to time. But, as the saying goes, we do not have to let them build a nest there.

PART THREE

Co-Creating with Your

Wise Inner Counselor™

Reflection 11

WELCOMING THE URGE TO CREATE

Your Wise Inner Counselor may send you on wild adventures into the unknown of your own untapped creative ingenuity.

Into the Misty Unknown

The Wise Inner Counselor is supremely practical. However, that practicality may appear as just the opposite when inner guidance forces us out of the box of what we consider normal, into the misty realm of what is novel, untried, untested and unfamiliar.

What the True Self knows that our outer awareness does not is that the shortest distance between where we are in consciousness and where we need to be is not a straight line.

It is, however, a very purposeful journey which requires us to consider the creative potential of our soul. That potential may never have occurred to us because to follow its path means accepting that we were born to create.

Out with the Old, in with the New

Before the start of class for the management course I taught on critical thinking and creative problem solving, I decorated the classroom walls with large posters containing quotes from artists, scientists and deep thinkers who expressed various aspects of the creative process. My favorite was from Pablo Picasso: "Every creative act is first of all an act of destruction." [7]

At first glance, a radical thought—until we consider how Nature operates. Only after being dormant for several months do green shoots emerge in springtime and blossom in summer. Their fruits are harvested in autumn and, when winter comes again, what remains of their former glory withers and dies.

If we plant perennials, we trust that they will come up in the spring. We also expect that our local nursery will supply our annual flower beds with all the variety and color we could wish for.

When we plant bulbs in the fall, we do not see them. They are under ground, waiting for warmer, longer days to urge them up through late spring snows to bloom. In the meantime, the world appears bleak and sorely lacking in the creative spark of life.

Creativity Naturally Disturbs the Status Quo

We like to think of creativity as being spontaneously uplifting, fun and renewing. It can be all that. It is also likely to demand that we extend ourselves outside of our comfort zones into a twilight space that seems chaotic, even dangerous.

This is the white page, the blank canvas, the unheard melody that every creative person faces at the beginning of a new project. It is also the hungry children, the yet-to-be-planned menu, the empty pot and the collection of raw ingredients that every family cook faces before the next meal's preparation begins.

In other words, the former state of past accomplishment or awareness must be completed, then pass away for the new to emerge—even when the project is as familiar as making dinner. There must be a blank page, an empty canvas, a composer's silent studio, a pot waiting to be filled. Otherwise, there is no room for the next expression of creativity's native abundance.

In those moments, when we listen with a receptive ear and heart, the Wise Inner Counselor is present, offering its unique inspiration for how we can fill the emptiness with Love in action—because it is the nature of Love to create something new, to extend itself, to go beyond where it was, perhaps only a minute earlier.

Why Do We Create?

I asked this question of students in my critical thinking classes. The opinion of many people in the course was that creativity caused more problems than it solved.

"It's disruptive," they would say. "Let a little bit of creativity loose in your organization and you lose control."

However, they also agreed that creating is what we humans do. We cannot help ourselves. We begin each day with a certain amount of energy and we create with it.

We make works of art or items like tools or clothing. We innovate systems and processes or start entire businesses. We also create environments from the emotions (positive or negative) that we bring to any situation.

And, of course, we create our lives. Each day we decide what we will make of life by the attitude we bring to our circumstances, whether or not we are pleased with how life is showing up for us at the moment.

The point is that we create because our souls are born to get things done in whatever way is most in alignment with our unique talents and under the direction of our Wise Inner Counselor.

To live is to create. And if a soul is denied the opportunity to manifest its gifts in the world, a part of that soul dies.

How Do We Create?

That, of course, is a perennial question. The answer is as unique as identifying exactly how each person will express their soul's urge to be more of the True Self today than it was the day before.

No two individuals will create the same—not if they are truly following their inner guidance and trusting that any initial uncertainty is an opportunity to step into the empty space of unknowing.

This is where the Wise Inner Counselor delights in showing up with a smile and an enthusiastic wave of its cosmic hand, inviting us to follow the story it cannot wait to share about how fulfilling life can be.

Here is the cradle of new ideas, innovations, inventions— whatever is most important for the soul to bring into form at that point of time. Because in the creation of every new manifestation, the soul grows in wisdom and in the power to be more insightful, loving and in sync with inner guidance.

'Tis a bold journey.

Reflection 12

SUMMONING THE STRENGTH TO CREATE

Though not easy, diving into your own manner of being creative can be enriching and fulfilling.

Creativity Takes Work

Anyone who has created a lesson plan for their homeschoolers or composed a purchase proposal for reluctant management or led a business innovation knows that effort is required.

Accomplished performers, athletes and stars in any profession make their feats appear easy. But the facility they demonstrate is built upon years of study and practice.

I once heard a story about the great Italian tenor, Luciano Pavarotti. He was greeting fans backstage after one of his thrilling concerts when a young man exclaimed to him, "Oh, Maestro, I would give my life to sing like that." Pavarotti looked him in the eye and said simply, "I did."

What Kind of Strength?

Over the years I have read many books on creativity. Two that have remained on my shelf are *The Courage to Create* by the late psychoanalyst Rollo May and *The War of Art* by best-selling author Steven

Pressfield. Before reviewing either volume, I was prompted to consider the content promised by their book covers.

Dr. May said that creativity is our healthiest impulse. He believed that all geniuses have a particular quality in common and that we can acquire creative courage. These are concepts with which I am familiar because I have taught them.

Pressfield's book is subtitled *Break Through the Blocks and Win Your Inner Creative Battles*. One reviewer described it as a "kick in the pants guaranteed to galvanize every would-be artist, visionary, or entrepreneur."

That is an approach to creativity I have not taught, although it is one that I live. I often need a boot in the behind if I am going to accomplish anything useful on a given day. Fortunately, my Wise Inner Counselor is very good at administering the boot.

As a writer, I work alone at home with multiple distractions available at any hour of the day or night. "Should I do some laundry? What's for lunch? Oh, look, the dining table is dusty." One of my favorite quotes about creativity attributed to John Steinbeck, states, "The hardest thing about writing is cleaning the refrigerator."

So, what kind of strength is necessary for us to access our healthiest impulse and do battle with our inner blocks? In my experience, what is required is nothing less than each day's full energy of mind, body and soul and the vigor of a courageous heart.

What Kind of Battles?

Innovating can be a battle when you are up against entrenched forces that are determined to defend the status quo. And don't we all have those forces within us?

I know I do. Over the years I have become very aware of those resistances that arise to distract, delay, depress or derail my creative ventures. Starting a new project always involves breaking trail through a jungle of uncertainty. And sometimes we do have to show up fully armed.

Pressfield says that resistance is the enemy. My perspective is that resistance is the symptom of a deeper, more sinister adversary—the not-self, that fabrication of identity which is comprised of the disowned, dissociated, unhealthy parts of our psychology.

These aspects of the lesser self may have been useful at one time as childhood defenses against the dangers we perceived in our environment. However, they now form an unconscious operating system that thwarts the Wise Inner Counselor whose purpose is to bring into the world of form our most profound reality.

A Common Misconception

When we first embark upon being more creative, we may bump into the belief that because we are made in the image of a divine creator, coming up with the next great idea should be easy.

Or we mistake ourselves for the doer rather than the willing receiver of inspiration and inner guidance—a mindset that can lead to disappointment when we discover that our egoistic "trying" is not leading to the spectacular results we had hoped for.

Following the Story

The more tenaciously I follow my Wise Inner Counselor, the more certain I am that an ideal matrix for any inner-directed project exists at refined levels of awareness, and that my job is to tune into that form and bring it into the physical.

This applies not only to my creative projects, but also to my desire to become more of my True Self every day.

When it came time for me to write the fourth of my spiritual romance novels, I felt inadequate to the task. How was I going to pull together all of the story lines and characters that had emerged from the three previous novels?

Fortunately, my Wise Inner Counselor came to my rescue with a simple solution: "Follow the story." Inner guidance seemed to be saying that the story already existed as a sort of etheric ideal that would reveal itself to me if I allowed it to take me on the adventure whose conclusion I could not see at the beginning.

I did follow the story and experienced many exciting *Eureka!* moments when each new plot twist came to light. Writing this book was a more obvious collaboration with the unseen world of my True Self than most of my other books.

Or perhaps they all have been that collaborative and I was not paying such close attention to how perfectly I am guided.

The Real Purpose of Creativity

When we summon every power within us to engage in the creative process, we can be sure of one thing: When the project is complete, we will not be the same as when we started.

I believe that is creativity's real purpose—to take us deeper into our own inner reality, to bring us closer to our own ideal, to carve away the rough or unsuitable elements of the false self that obstruct our best creative ventures.

We become like Michelangelo, who described his sculpting as carving away all of the stone that was not the figure he perceived locked in the block of marble. His creations (like the *Pietà* or his

David) exude a vitality that makes me think he sensed a hidden life force within the stone that longed to be liberated.

Waiting to Be Freed

I believe our soul is like that. It is locked in the hardened substance of the false self that we have concretized around us. The soul is waiting to be freed by a cosmic sculptor whose voice urges us to see with finer eyes the beautiful creature we really are.

The good news is that the trapped life force, which originated as soul energy, wants to participate in its own liberation. While the largely unconscious structures of the false self may mount a mighty resistance to the True Self, the life force that has been misqualified in negative patterns leaps to the fore when we summon the resolve to follow inner guidance and replace those useless patterns of thought, feeling and action with practical, positive ones.

Joyful Warriors

Although becoming your True Self can feel like magic, we know that the final outcome is the result of a lot of hard work. We must plow many fields and plant many seeds before the fruits of our efforts ripen to the harvest.

And I believe there is another point to make here.

We must always remember that the Wise Inner Counselor speaks to us out of its own communion with Love.

The surge of joy we feel at the completion of a job well done is that energy which infuses all of our best efforts with the power to share a transformative energy with our audience—whether that audience is a worldwide community or a well-fed family with tummies warmed by our creative expertise in the kitchen.

When we remember that it is Love which gives the increase to what we have planted and watered with our best efforts, I am certain that the strength we summon to undo the enemy of the True Self will be that of joyful warriors.

Reflection 13

Enhancing Your Creativity

Your own creativity is a naturally healthy
process. How will you nurture it?

Suggestions from Life and Learning

These several ways of encouraging your creativity are the result of many conversations, classes and personal experiences shared over years of exploration and discovery with colleagues, friends and course attendees.

1. Embrace the Twilight

Ned Herrmann, developer of Whole Brain® Technology, discovered that he got his best ideas when his brain was resting in Theta, the twilight state between waking and sleeping. This brain state is the home of those great ideas that evaporate if you do not write them down when they wake you at 3:00 a.m.[8]

Observe yourself. What puts you in Theta? Take a walk. Take a shower. Go for a drive. Play with your animals. Go to an art gallery. Or a concert. Surround yourself with vital sights, sounds, aromas, textures, tastes, physical sensations—and see what causes you to lift off into that unselfconscious space that is purely present.

TIP: Activities that engage arms and legs moving in opposition stimulate both sides of the brain. Walking, running, jogging, cross-country skiing, T'ai Chi, Qigong or dancing are effective. Brain Gym® is one of the best. [9]

2. Observe Your Meditation Practice

Notice if your practice contributes to useful inspiration, or do you tend to space out? If you are more spacey than inspired, you might experiment with different options.

Meditative states can also arise in listening to the sounds of Nature or to silence itself, following the breath and the mindful practice of paying deep attention to the present moment. Experiment with various forms of meditation to discover what best leads you into the creative flow of inner guidance.

3. Carve Out Time for Creative Activities

You cannot force creativity. Ask any artist or writer who has ever had artist's or writer's block. Your mind feels like a desert. No matter how hard you try, you get no ideas. No inspiration. Nothing.

However, a key observation about creativeness, made by famed psychologist Abraham Maslow, is that achieving absorption into what he called "the matter-in-hand" can spark inspiration, novel solutions or peak experiences that lead to a state of awareness that transcends the outer self.

TRY THIS: Remember a time when you were so absorbed in an activity that you became unaware of anything else going on. What did that feel like? What were you doing or not doing? Could you include more of that in your daily life?

Here is another key to unlocking your creativity: Do not worry about performing or perfecting. Just noodle. Allow yourself to go childlike and play.

This is the "dance like no one is watching" approach.
Have fun and see what creative sparks emerge.

4. Get Out into Nature

My two favorite poet-philosophers, William Wordsworth and John O'Donohue, discovered profound creative inspiration in Nature.

They each lived in the "thin places" of England and Ireland where mystery inhabits the very soil of the land, the mist in the air and the sound of the sea. They were also great walkers who spent many hours in deep communion with the outer landscape that led them to plumb the mysteries of the inner one.

Of course, there are "thin places" all over the world. Your heart is one of them when you open it to the unique "is-ness" of Nature herself.

Pay deep attention to rivers and streams, rocks and mountains, valleys and glens, tall grasses and tiny lichen. Breath in the scent of harmony abiding in even the tiniest plot of grass and feel yourself transported into the transcendence of Nature's wisdom.

5. Create a Hospitable Environment

One thing I have learned from my own experience as a writer and an instructor is that creativity is environmentally sensitive.

What I mean is that not all environments are conducive to initiating creative expression. Of course, when the poetical juices are flowing, I can write just about anywhere. In fact, noisy airports and restaurants have provided some of my most insightful poetry.

However, if you want to increase your creativity, I suggest that you pay attention to what sort of environments are especially stimulating to fresh ideas and perspectives.

A mentor once told me that Walt Disney had four separate offices which he used for different types of work. That makes sense to me. There is one particular setting in my house where I do nearly all of my original writing. Editing and other computer work usually happens in my office. If I reach an impasse, I go for a walk, take a drive or a bath. And if my brain is weary of words, words, words, I watch a movie or visit an art gallery.

> **TRY THIS:** If you are feeling stuck or low on inspiration, consider a practice that worked for a famous advertising editor. He is reported to have taken a different route to work every day of his career. His commute was less than thirty minutes, but he managed to find unique passages through side streets and alleys as a means of stimulating his eye and imagination with novel sights and sounds that he otherwise would not have experienced.

6. Create a Vision Board or Scrapbook

If writing is not your preference, you might want to create a kind of physical journal like a vision board, collage of photos, scrapbook,

Vision boards can be any size or shape.

or slide show of videos and still images. Audios are also a lot of fun.

Carrying a sketch book or your phone with you is a great tool for capturing unexpected sights and sounds of life.

The point is to do whatever provides your soul with an opportunity to communicate its deepest longings. Even if you are a writer, including some visual aids or recording audios can trigger insights that you would otherwise pass by.

One reason journaling of any kind works as a creative practice is that putting your thoughts and feelings on paper gets them out of your head and into the physical where you can see them. They become objects that are no longer running your life. You can decide to keep or discard the thought or feeling and move on from there.

> **TRY THIS:** Before you begin, pose a question such as: "What do I need to know right now?" Then open yourself to what comes. The goal is to give expression to what in you needs to be given life in the space you have provided.

The response from your Wise Inner Counselor can emerge in any number of ways that include encouragement, comfort, creative solutions and spiritual inspiration.

Neither flattering nor critical, inner guidance always speaks on behalf of your highest good and may surprise you with options you never conceived of before asking for its guidance.

7. Associate with Creative People

One reason I sometimes enjoy writing in crowded places is that I find the group energy stimulating. The setting may not provide inspiration for content, but the movement of bodies and minds can urge me past a feeling of being stuck.

> **TRY THIS:** Consider spending time with people who share your creative interests. For example, I knew a pro-

fessor of English who used to conduct a writing group.

Several of us would meet at a coffee shop and spend no more than eight minutes in conversation. Then we would be silent for the next hour as everybody worked on their own project.

I found this to be a very rich experience in the contagious atmosphere of creativity. In the discussion that followed, nearly everyone remarked on the shared energy that flowed within and around the group.

We offered suggestions if they were wanted and usually ended up bouncing ideas off of one another in an impromptu brainstorming session.

People in any profession can gather like this. Try it sometime with your colleagues and see what happens.

Reflection 14

WHAT DOES IT MEAN TO BE A CO-CREATOR?

*We are learning that creating means giving all that
we are and more than we ever thought we could be.*

The Nature of the Partnership

To be a co-creator with the presence of Love is to enter into a
partnership that is uncompromising in its expectations of us and
beyond generous in its support of the outcomes of which our Wise
Inner Counselor knows we are capable.

Just as our True Self urges us to embrace the spiritual realms
that exist within us, when we commit to being a co-creator with
the truth of our being, we must answer that call with equal determination and intensity to take the proffered hand of inner guidance.

Do We Take Creativity for Granted?

I often think of the famous image Michelangelo painted on the
Sistine Chapel. Adam is reclining. To me he seems rather laid back,
barely deigning to extend his arm while God is fervently reaching
out to touch the man's finger with the enlivening energy of creation.

Too often, I think we are like Adam in that painting—blithely
going about our daily lives, expecting that a magical presence will

touch us with divine inspiration with very little effort on our parts. In my experience, being a co-creator does not work that way.

Rather, the process requires equal commitment on both sides of the relationship. Although that may appear an impossible task, we give our best effort every day.

At the same time, we realize that the Wise Inner Counselor will always exceed us in vision and innovative ideas—which is why we listen so intently for its inspiration and guidance.

However, we do not use that knowledge as an excuse to stop striving. Because the goal and our soul's greatest desire is to unite with our Wise Inner Counselor. Above all, we want to become that essence of truth, beauty and goodness so we can walk the earth as Love embodied in action.

Never-Ending Opportunities

Practicing co-creatorship is the surest way I know to achieve that union. Creativity offers never-ending opportunities for integrating our spirituality and our humanity—which is what becoming the True Self is all about.

When we accept the circumstances that our commitment to co-creating presents, there will always be the next project—the one that will be the most challenging thing we have ever done.

That endeavor will always demand more love, more wisdom, more strength than we thought we were capable of offering to our partner—until, with the guidance of our Wise Inner Counselor, we actually do cross the finish line.

Then, miraculously, or so it seems, as we achieve that next turn on what can be viewed as the spiral of life transcending life, we find ourselves functioning at a new level of awareness.

We Will Be Changed

Once upon a time somebody may have told us that when we embark upon the path of co-creatorship we will never be the same. At that time we probably didn't quite believe them. Now we do. Although we may not clearly recall the steps we have climbed or the valleys of doubt and fear we have traversed to reach where we are now, we know we have changed.

And perhaps recollection of the past doesn't really matter.

What does matter is that we are not who or what we were. Our perspective has altered. We look out at the landscape with the distinct impression that our True Self is seeing that world through our eyes. Or rather, we are viewing the world through the eyes of our True Self, through the lens of an accelerated consciousness that we have only now attained.

Contemplating that Oneness

Sometimes the changes my Wise Inner Counselor effects in me are so subtle that I do not realize until later than an inner alchemy has been taking place over a period of time—almost at a cellular level.

I used to experience my True Self as an outside force that I had to reach out or up for. Or whose guidance would come sailing in as if from an external source.

But these days I have a physical, sensory, felt sense of being enfolded in and permeated by a presence of inner reality that used to come and go, and that now seems right at home where I am.

I know that my Wise Inner Counselor desires that each day will become for me an aspirational experience of penetrating deeper into the mystery of being and what it actually means to be real, to be in tune with my highest principles.

What If We Had No Resistance?

I know that every True Self in this universe is urging us to keep growing, to continue allowing more light energy into our awareness. Because the path of soul freedom really is one of allowing.

If we had no resistance to light, we would be all light. If we had no resistance to Love, we would be all Love.

The Wise Inner Counselor knows what that means for each of us and daily inspires us to release our souls from the bondage of useless patterns of thought, feeling and behavior.

This is the alchemy of refinement we are called upon to engage as the inner work behind our outer work. The two function simultaneously, each supporting each. One enhancing the other.

Oneness Can Happen

My experience shows me that when we accept the totality of being a co-creative partner with our Wise Inner Counselor, this oneness can be the result.

What began as our perception of two partners—one spiritual and one material—now merges into a single individual in whom being and doing are functioning in the perpetual reciprocity of a dynamic wholeness. We enter into that wholeness and behold ourselves as astonishingly real, now more able than ever before to continually transcend the lesser self.

The path that leads to an unfettered future of joyful creativity is what I have come to call our Soul Poetics™.

Reflection 15

STEPPING INTO THE BEAUTY OF YOUR SELF WITH SOUL POETICS

Your True Self is naturally beautiful. How you
express that beauty is your Soul Poetics.

Every Soul Is Poetical

I first came upon the term "poetics" as used by John O'Donohue, when he included it as the chapter title "Work as a Poetics of Growth" in his insightful book *Anam Cara: A Book of Celtic Wisdom.*[10]

While "poetics" is usually defined as a treatise on a literary work, here I believe he meant to consider work as a deep expression of soul purpose—manifesting through what a person creates as they weave the tapestry of their lives. In other words, as their Soul Poetics.

The root word for "poetry" means "to create." Therefore, Soul Poetics is both what we create and how we do it. It relates to what we make of our lives in consonance with our Wise Inner Counselor and what we bring into form in the process.

Soul Poetics Lives in the Fluid Present

Your life is a moving stream that is never quite the same as it was the minute or hour or day before. When philosopher Heraclitus said,

"You could not step twice in the same river," this is what he meant.[11]

The idea of the fluid present comes from a concept held by early Christian mystics. They called it the *nunc fluens* or "flowing now." In this state of "present-ness," the past is preserved while thoughts of the future can also be entertained.

Whether we are thinking about a past, current or future event, that mental image is in the present. As thought and experience flow, so does the present moment—the *nunc fluens*.

I have found that sitting by a moving stream or, ideally, along the Atlantic Ocean's Irish coast (shown here) while paying attention to my body's response is a profound way to tune in to my Wise Inner Counselor, moment by fluid moment.

Contacting the Sweetness of Soul Poetics

I have done many hours of meditation and journaling around the idea of Soul Poetics. I find it to be ephemeral, not easy to define. It must be lived to be fully understood.

Perhaps one reason is that our souls are a bit shy. They resist the spotlight. Instead, they prefer to reveal themselves indirectly under the guidance and protection of the True Self. So I find it not surprising that when I experience my Wise Inner Counselor speaking on behalf of my soul, greater clarity of the depth of Soul Poetics comes to me softly and sweetly.

By way of describing this ineffable concept, the following pages are the result of resting in the gentle presence of what inner wisdom wishes to convey to me. For example:

Your Soul Poetics is the essence of your being. It is the heart place where your spirituality and your humanity unite to transform the world.

Soul Poetics connects to your greatness. It is what you most desire to create in your life and how you are inspired to create it.

Your Soul Poetics is a calling. Infinitely fertile and expressive, it urges you to develop the inner sight and hearing of your Wise Inner Counselor's presence.

Soul Poetics awakens inner wisdom as the voice of your True Self speaking for all that is good and true and beautiful in you. This communion creates a bridge between the Unseen and the seen, connecting you with something greater than yourself.

Your Soul Poetics encompasses your best efforts and finest innate qualities. It opens the way to Love's great mysteries in you. The poetics of your soul is how you are Love—as only you can be it.

Meditating on Soul Poetics as Beauty

When the concept of Soul Poetics first came into my awareness, it appeared as a sort of "knowing" that the soul is beautiful and that

Beauty is an essence which pervades all true expressions of the soul. My muse really took off with this tangible insight into the nature of my Self. That still happens whenever my attention rests softly in that inner space.

I offer these musings as an invitation for you to meditate with your soul and discover the unique way in which a deep quality of Beauty evokes the truth of your being.

Beauty rests in the "is-ness" of being. This is what the poet Wordsworth meant about "seeing into the life of things."

Beauty is the joy of young animals at play, frolicking in the sheer exuberance of being alive.

Beauty is sensory. It is the fragrance of truth, the touch of goodness, the pure light energy of all that is spiritual.

Beauty emanates from the community when its members are held in honor and respect.

To recognize the intrinsic beauty of someone is to let them be, to allow them to develop into who or what they are meant to be.

Beauty is in the eye of the beholder when that eye has been purified of negativity that clouds its perception.

The soul's original world is supremely beautiful. Witnessing even a glimpse of its exquisite radiance brings tears to the eyes and ecstasy to the heart.

Although Beauty is not form, its ethereal essence radiates through balanced forms. It is a presence with a purpose—to free humanity from all manner of darkness, despair and disillusion.

Beauty arrests the mind—stilling it, opening its portals of perception, quieting its questioning nature and filling it with a knowing of sacred things that cannot be touched by the mundane.

Beauty resides in the gracious eye that receives, nurtures, protects and transmits clear seeing to others whose sight may be gently opened to Creation's innate perfection.[12]

What Living a Life of Soul Poetics Can Be Like

Finally, here are some experiences which I and others have had as we have embraced the inspiration of Soul Poetics in our lives.

- Life takes on a magical quality as the details of living and working turn out better.

- You become more authentically yourself.

- Relationships improve as outworn habits fall away.

- Loss offers greater understanding of life and becomes a gateway to higher consciousness.

- Inner sight and hearing emerge as inspired states of refined awareness.

- You develop hospitality toward life's ups and downs.

- Your life is transformed daily as you collaborate with inner guidance and your unique talents are realized.

Discover Your Sense of Purpose with Soul Poetics

As you offer your gifts and talents to life, the star of your True Self shines brighter.

Soul Poetics can lead to self-transcendence, an experience distinguished by those transformative moments when some part of you moves away from its standing as one thing to become another.

Expressing your Soul Poetics is key to living a fulfilling life. It is how you become more genuinely yourself with every passing day. It is also how you do the great work described in this book's companion publication. [13]

To conclude this reflection, I offer the following poem which emerged as an early realization that my soul knows more about the future than my outer self can perceive.

A Glimmering Sense of Purpose

To embark upon the inner journey
is to open a door frequented by dreamers.

Spirit is eager for your company
and rushes in to carry you aloft
on this new adventure
whose fulfillment waits upon your will.

The soul knows what she's doing
and gladly packs her bags.
Your ancient calling beckons—
the voyage has begun.[14]

Soul Poetics as a Source of Healing

We all have issues with people in our lives.
Engaging in the work you were born for
can lead to resolution of those issues.

Deep Resolution with Soul Poetics

There are no perfect parents, just as there are no perfect children. We likely have known each other in past lives, and we have things to work out in this one.

In my case, the issue that Soul Poetics helped resolve was with my human mother and with what many call the Divine Mother or the World Mother.

When I first began seriously writing poetry in early 2015, I was doing a lot of psychological processing. My mother had passed away only eighteen months prior, and hers had been a difficult death that was hard on both of us. So hard, in fact, that I had not written a word since she died.

However, when a friend told me that April was known as "write-a-poem-a-day month," I decided to take up the challenge. Poems began to flow, and many of them were about my mother.

I published some of them in my book *Poetics of Soul & Fire.*

Many others I did not keep or publish. They were too personal. The process of writing them was all that mattered for my inner work.

An Inner Journey with Soul Poetics

The poems of April continued through May and June and July. By that time I had realized that being a poet was an essential element of my life's purpose which I had not actively explored before.

As I settled deeply into writing, I found myself communing with my soul as a feminine aspect of my being. And I remembered a wise woman saying that for anyone to merge with their True Self, they must come to terms with their own feminine nature, even when residing in a masculine body.

I was definitely in the thick of that process.

I loved the state of consciousness that poetry led me into. I was encouraged by the deep psychological resolution I discovered when I allowed my soul to speak her peace in verse.

This process came to dramatic fruition as I was writing my third collection of inspirational poetry titled *Idylls from the Garden of Spiritual Delights & Healing*.

These verses were different. Rather than stand-alone poems, the entire book was a poetical journey of a soul who is making her way through the garden of Gaia, a manifestation of the World Mother who lives in the etheric level of the Unseen.

As my own soul traversed Gaia's garden, I discovered that in order to write these poems I had to find a deeper sense of resolution with that feminine presence in the person of my human mother and with several significant figures in my life who were also women.

Awash in Waves of Forgiveness

The process caught me by surprise. At first, I had thought I was merely writing poems that included angels, fairies, magical beings and elemental nature spirits such as sylphs of the air, undines of the water, gnomes of the earth and fiery spirits called salamanders.

However, as the story progressed, my soul went deep into issues of resistance to the Mother. One day when I was working on a poem about Gaia, something broke loose in me and I began to sob great floods of tears as I asked the World Mother and the spirit of my deceased mother to forgive me for causing the seen and unseen mothers a lot of heartache due to my actions that had not come from my True Self.

The experience was brief and yet very profound as I felt waves of forgiveness wash through my being. I was changed forever. And I am certain that the main reason is because I was so completely engaged in my Soul Poetics.

Focusing on Our Purpose in Life

When we are totally focused on some aspect of the work we were born for, our soul is able to attract inspiration and illumination—energies which then pull the soul up even higher in vibration into more refined levels of awareness and being.

One outcome of this accelerating consciousness can be great work. Here is the weaving of being and doing that lies at the center of life in the world of time and space.

Ireland Enhanced the Process

Spending time in Ireland has always inspired new poetry. Visits to the Emerald Isle have never failed to deepen my relationship with my soul, my Soul Poetics and the Mother.

I believe one reason for this experience is that Ireland is the land of the Goddess Brigid, who is said to have brought the rainbow to Éire in ancient times. In the sixth century there was also a human bishop known as Saint Brigid who founded a dual monastery that admitted both men and women.

Ireland is filled with springs and wells, reputed to be openings into the body of the goddess. For those with soul sensitivity to these manifestations, the feminine energy is palpable.

I cannot help but feel that her tangible presence is one reason why many people flock to Ireland each year and why, almost without exception, they remark that arriving feels as if they have come home. The Mother's hospitality is legendary in Ireland, and I believe that her comforting care is a quality our souls long for.

For me, being my True Self has a lot of do with embodying the poetics of my feminine soul on behalf of my progress on the spiritual path and in helping others whom I meet along the way.

I have found this to be the case for women and men alike.

My photo of the statue of Brigid the Bishop located in
Kildare, Ireland. She is holding the eternal flame
which she lit at her dual monastery in the sixth century.

Reflection 17

Weaving Your Humanity and Your Spirituality

*Partnership with the Wise Inner Counselor
enables and accelerates the process.*

Why Are We Here?

Our innate abilities—our Soul Poetics—are what we most desire to actualize in life and work.

These gifts are what we came to earth to contribute as only we can. This is our purpose that glimmers—perhaps unseen in our early days, yet profoundly felt in the heart as our reason for being.

Some souls know from the cradle what they are meant to be, and they pursue an unwavering trajectory into medicine or science or the arts or the trades or parenthood.

Others come to a well-defined purpose later in life, through experience in various careers and areas of endeavor. And yet, seen in retrospect, the thread of purpose was probably always present—perhaps as a medical professional or caregiver, a master craftsman or business owner, a manager, athlete or member of the military.

As I discovered through years of teaching, in many instances a person's soul gifts are transferable abilities that come to the fore in multiple situations—until the individual at last declares:

"I see now! Here is the gift I feel most urgently called to bring to life!" And in that moment, the Wise Inner Counselor responds:

> *Yes! Let us make the most of these talents and apply them consciously to the days that remain—whether they be long or short. For in this doing on behalf of the world is the being of the soul enhanced. Here is the moment when your humanity and your spirituality weave together as Love in action.*

Descartes' Mistake

We may think that doing our best in the world of work does not require spirituality. Indeed, a materialistic education and societal pressures may try to convince us that the human mind is sufficient to any task.

But we who have learned to rely upon the voice of inner guidance for inspiration, direction and warning (and correction when our actions have led us astray) know better.

We have learned that Descartes had it backwards when he asserted, "*Cogito, ergo sum*—I think, therefore I am."

The truth is that I am, therefore I have the capacity to think. If I am wise, which I desire to be, I will lean my human mind in to the thoughts of my True Self. Then my purpose in all aspects of life will become clear.

The Desire for Something More

For many souls, life is sufficiently satisfying because their work affords them the opportunity to actualize their innate talents.

Then there are others who sense the potential for something more. For them the voice of inner wisdom speaks of deeper, wider, more refined states of consciousness. And they run to greet those levels of awareness as the ultimate, spiritual purpose for which they were born. Who knows? You may be one of them.

Transcending Our Great Work

Discovering our life's calling can precipitate unexpected opportunities for self-mastery, particularly when we approach any task before us as more than a job.[15]

In that context, any work can be great work.

Likewise, our Soul Poetics is more than what we are here to create and how we create it. It is also the process by which we can transcend even our greatest work in the material realm and step into the spiritual reality where we are true to our Self.

Stephen Eckl contemplating the unity of his spirituality and his humanity at Jenny Lake, Grand Teton National Park, Wyoming.

PART FOUR

Being True
to Your Self

IN SEARCH OF A HEALTHY PSYCHOLOGY

*The True Self desires our understanding
of the psyche—the psychology of the soul.*

Finding a Way Forward

In 2009 I was in a quandary about my future. What would become
of me now that my husband had left this world? I had worked in
a number of careers, including business course development and
training. I had lived in a spiritual community where Stephen and I
met. But now, nothing from my past was calling me forward.

At the time, I was developing and presenting workshops for
the educational arm of The Denver Hospice. I also attended several
conferences on grief and end-of-life issues where I associated with
professionals who were counselors and educators. Nearly all of
them had advanced degrees in various branches of psychology.

Inner guidance suggested that I take up this course of study.

Searching for Soul Psychology

I had always been interested in psychology, but not in its abnormal-
ities. Surely, I thought, there must be a way to study the psyche in a
state of oneness, not fragmentation.

An Internet search revealed the term "transpersonal psychology" and an accredited academic institute[16] to answer the question
that had burned in my mind for years: How can I become more
whole so I can help others do the same?

I immediately enrolled in this program. One of my first happy
discoveries was that prominent psychologists, led by Dr. Abraham
H. Maslow, had been on the same search for a healthy psychology. In
fact, he is the one who coined the term "transpersonal psychology."

Filling in the Healthy Half of Psychology

Throughout the 1960s, Maslow and several of his colleagues were
developing innovative theories in response to psychoanalysis and
behaviorism, which dismissed and even pathologized crucial dimensions of human experience such as spirituality and alternate states
of consciousness, often referred to as peak experiences.

Instead, Maslow began focusing primarily on psychological
health as opposed to pathology. He wrote that: "It is as if Freud has
supplied to us the sick half of psychology, and we must now fill it
out with the healthy half." [17]

A Philosophical Scientist

I wish I had known Dr. Maslow. His lectures and notes, collected
in *The Farthest Reaches of Human Nature*, reveal a man of humor, acute
powers of observation and a genuine love of people.

He has been described as a philosophical scientist because
of his move beyond the value-free, mechanical approach to human
psychology practiced by the schools of thought which preceded
him. He advocated an approach that identified the psychologist or
analyst as a non-interfering observer of a person's behavior, not the
controller of it.

His words indicate a deep, yet practical thinker who joyfully
followed the leadings of his own Wise Inner Counselor. His theories
continued to evolve until the very end of his life as he proved in

his own existence the value and satisfaction of transcending today what one has grasped the day before.

A Balm to My Soul

This positive approach to the psyche was a balm to my soul as I shuddered to recall the college freshman psychology course I was required to take in 1968, around the same time that Maslow was developing his most advanced theories.

The psychology department at my school was run by professors who taught the behaviorist theories of B. F. Skinner. Our lab sessions consisted of testing pigeons to see if they would still go after food even when they got an electric shock along with the food.

To me these labs were nothing but animal cruelty. I remember taking one pitiful bird back to its cage after a testing session. The poor thing was limp as a rag from all the shocks it had received.

Validating My Transpersonal Perspective

Now, at last, I had found a compassionate psychology that fostered a desire to help people grow into the full human beings they were meant to be. What a relief!

I was thrilled with this course of study because it validated the mystical experiences I'd had since I was a child, mostly as a result of listening to the promptings of my Wise Inner Counselor and from being on a spiritual path of self-discovery for several decades.

Many of my fellow students had experienced similar mystical states and were likewise spiritually oriented. We were grateful that our program agreed with the great mystical traditions of East and West which teach that human beings of any age have the capacity to be transported out of their everyday awareness.

Those experiences may be as simple as a brief *a-ha!* moment of personal discovery all the way to states of cosmic consciousness where they understand what William Blake meant when he wrote:

To see a World in a Grain of Sand
And a Heaven in a Wild Flower,
Hold Infinity in the palm of your hand
And Eternity in an hour.

The fact that peak experiences caused individuals' sense of self to extend beyond the personal to encompass wider aspects of humankind, life, psyche—even the Universe—meant that their worldview became more expansive.

Even after a peak experience was over, they would tend to see themselves in more holistic or global terms. Their experiences were trans (beyond) personal, and their way of being in the world improved.

Opening the Way to Personal Growth

Like my classmates and me, the early transpersonal psychologists were fascinated by the fact that, although peak experiences were often no more than flashes of insight, they seemed to leave behind an essence of magnanimity, compassion and selflessness that permanently elevated the experiencers' way of being so that personal growth became their primary motivation.

The people they observed began to consciously work on transcending their present state of awareness in order to transform the elevated states of consciousness that occur in peak experiences into actual stages of psychological development that could become a way of being, rather than a fleeting moment of exaltation.

Who or What Triggers a Peak Experience?

These transcendent events have a way of enfolding us in an orb of cosmic potential that is both universal and personal—qualities that I associate with the finest aspects of our innermost being.

I have a profound sense that the greatest desire of our Wise Inner Counselor is to accelerate our soul's progress on the path of self-realization by giving us a vivid taste of the universal wholeness that encompasses all and transcends all. In those moments, we become the totality of the radiance we perceive.

No one knows when a peak experience will occur. That is the brilliance of cosmic timing. The surprise of the event is part of its gift that operates outside of linear time.

Then, for a timeless, spaceless interval we are infused with light energy and enfolded in Love and illumination. In this state where all that is noble, true and worthy seems possible, our soul desires to never go back to lesser levels of awareness.

The Ageless Impetus to Change

While a mature determination to follow a rigorous path of self-transcendence may develop later in life, the initial impetus for positive and permanent change can occur at an early age.

I know this to be true because I had a dramatically transformative peak experience when I was about nine years old.

A visit to my grandmother set the stage for this remarkable occurrence that remains as fresh in my mind today as it was then and which continues to comfort and inspire me.

Reflection 19

SOME MEMORIES NEVER FADE

*No matter how old you are, a peak experience can feel
like stepping into the transformative orb of another world.*

Glimpsing the Other Side of Life

Even as a very young child, I viewed my existence as a continuum
that moved from this life on to what philosopher William James
called "something more."

My family believed in an afterlife, but I thought my parents
were profoundly disinterested in what actually happened "over
there." I, however, found it fascinating to imagine a world beyond
the physical where people went when they died and where one day
I, too, might go.

I was especially intrigued by my Grandma Cody's near-death
experience that had left her with a gift of clairvoyance which the
family affectionately called her "hotline to God."

While lying gravely ill with child-bed fever after the birth of
her fourth child, she had heard what she described as angels sing-
ing outside her window and she'd felt a divine presence that stayed
with her throughout her life.

One summer, when I was about nine years old, we were at
Cody's house for lunch and she was saying grace in her quaint way:

"Now, Jesus, you take care of these dear children." (She always talked as if he were her best friend.)

With my head bowed and my eyes closed, I suddenly felt the room fill up with a radiant energy. Peeking around, I couldn't see anything, but I could feel it. And I silently announced to God, "I want what Grandma Cody has." She clearly had friends in heaven and I wanted them, too.

Later that summer, I got my first real glimpse of the other side of life. I was lazing on my swing set in our backyard, enjoying a balmy breeze, thinking intently about the fascinating book on ancient Greece I had been reading.

I was imagining the hot Aegean sun beating on my face, making diamonds of light on the azure-blue sea, with iridescent marble columns a short distance behind me. It was a scene so vivid I could almost remember being there—almost.

As I sat motionless on the swing, trying to will myself back to antiquity, I was transported. In my mind's eye I no longer saw the glistening white of Greek temples but, rather, a tunnel of light. With the vision came the clear idea that this was where both Jesus and Buddha came from and where they lived.

Although I had been raised with traditionally Christian beliefs, this concept did not seem strange. I had become familiar with the Buddha in my world history books, and my beliefs about Jesus were already expanding beyond Sunday school stories.

Neither of these great beings actually appeared in the tunnel I saw, but I instantly knew that they were there in the brilliant, white light that glowed in the center. I felt myself being comforted with a promise that if I would follow that light, one day I would remember ancient Greece—and much, much more.

As I grew up, although I did not see any more tunnels of light, I decided I was a mystic—a person who desires union with the Divine, however she defines it. In my late teens and early twenties, I had many experiences of synchronicity—unexplainable coincidences or serendipitous events that I ascribed to being in tune with angels or other spiritual beings.

I did my best to follow the light I had seen in the tunnel. Yet all the while, I felt a persistent inner hunger—an intense longing for the spiritual connectedness that seemed so natural to my grand-mother. Much later, I would come to realize that the presence in the tunnel was my Wise Inner Counselor, speaking to me as the voice of Love.[18]

Descriptions from My Transpersonal Classmates

While I was studying Transpersonal Psychology, I made a point of recording some vivid descriptions of peak experiences from others who had had them. (There were a lot of us in that program!)

My classmates all agreed that putting their experiences into words was difficult, but they obliged me with these attempts at describing the ineffable.

- Awesome. Beyond words.

- Time is lost and place disappears.

- That terrible, shame-based self-consciousness that so many humans suffer from evaporates in a blissful instant of Beyond Self.

- You cease to be critical of self or others as feelings of peace and joy take over.

- You are absorbed into Nature, with heightened percep-tion and a profound sense of the interconnectedness of all things.

- Spiraling into a cosmic flow, you lose all sense of a sepa-rate ego self as you slip into a state of oneness with the Divine and the entire universe.

"Inspiration" by artist Marie Antoinette Kelley

Reflection 20

Being Transpersonal

*Going beyond the former self is one of the
primary goals of a transpersonal perspective.*

Paying Attention to Peak Experiences

Many of us in my psychology program agreed that our peak experiences often led us to transcend the very career concerns we had
been working hard to achieve—exactly like many Eastern mystical
traditions whose goal is to transform or dissolve the former self.

In other words, although our worldly endeavors were important to us, we were motivated by values and ideals that had at least as
much to do with how we were being as with what we were doing.

We were seeking benefits beyond the purely personal through
the communion with inner wisdom that often occurred through
mystical or transpersonal experiences. We were identifying with
something greater than the purely individual self and were often
engaged in service to others.

Here again were the "being" aspects of life—just as my Wise
Inner Counselor had been directing me for years.

Reclaiming the Sacred

The transpersonal community was an interesting one. Just as I had found in the spiritual community where I had lived for nearly two decades, there was a general commonality of perspective that was comforting and stimulating, as many of my fellow students were actively striving to transcend their former selves.

Looking back now, I can see that the people in each community were very much alike. Both groups were (and are) intent on reclaiming the sacred nature of the psyche—the soul.

Without that perspective, we can observe the negative effects of a post-modern mindset that dismisses the existence of values and virtues—giving rise to a worldview that reduces the individual to an expendable cog in a mechanized society.

With this kind of thinking, it is no wonder that suicide rates are so high, especially in young people whose developing minds innately crave contact with experiences that will transport them to refined dimensions of unitive awareness.

For people who are naturally transpersonal, the psychological damage of having to endure a reductionist mentality is incalculable. Souls like ours know we are meant to develop and achieve our full potential. For us, being denied the opportunity to continually transcend ourselves is soul-killing.

Characteristics of Being Transpersonal

As I have continued to study the psychology of the soul, I have made some observations about what it means to take a transpersonal or self-transcendent approach to life.

When I have shared some of these observations with workshop participants, many have found them very helpful in identifying the dynamics of their own path of self-discovery. I invite you to consider these descriptions for yourself.

Self-transcenders are likely to identify themselves as spiritual but not religious, and they may follow the precepts of a mystical spirituality.

They are ecumenical in their approach to religion and are likely to be interested in the similarities between various traditions rather than the differences in dogmas.

Self-transcenders have an underlying faith in the universality of Spirit and are happiest when their life experience emanates from the point of unity between the spiritual and the material, between being and doing.

To self-transcenders, life is a sacred adventure that they approach with reverence and a determination to attain spiritual dimensions of consciousness. They are easily moved to tears when speaking of their experiences.

Self-transcenders may demonstrate a remarkable ability to be grounded in the common-sense realities of daily life while retaining a profound connection with their own spiritual essence of soul and inner wisdom.

Such people may demonstrate exceptional mastery over the things of this world. Connection with their Wise Inner Counselor prompts them to perceptions and actions that appear unavailable to those who operate from a strictly materialistic point of view.

Self-transcenders perceive life on a transpersonal path as a spiral. Their aim is to be continually accelerating to more refined levels of consciousness which lead them to states of transcendence that can become permanent stages of psychological and spiritual development.

Challenges of Being Transpersonal in Today's World

People who possess a truly transpersonal perspective can find it difficult to locate others who share the same intrinsic values such as truth, goodness, beauty, perfection or excellence—values which cannot be reduced to anything more fundamental.

The good news is that once these self-transcenders become aware of what makes them different from their families, friends or colleagues, they are more likely to relax, champion their own unique values and seek out others of like mind without feeling guilty for wanting more from their personal development.

While remaining mindfully grounded, the more that any of us aim to refine our consciousness, the more profound is the insight we can gain into our reason for being and how to become more of who we really are—our True Self.

A Caution About Leaping to Transpersonal

One of the most important concepts I was introduced to in my study of transpersonal psychology was the need to develop a strong sense of self before one can transcend that self.

We know that the personality we bring with us as we go through life can be burdened with past traumas or ways of thinking and acting that are no longer useful. However, it is also clear from the observations of Maslow and others that, as psychologist Jack Engler said, "You have to be somebody before you can be nobody."[19]

What he meant, and what the people I studied with were quick to emphasize, is that the transcendent realm of consciousness requires a developed strength of mind and character before one can actually exist in that rarefied atmosphere of the "beyond-personal."

To understand the situation, we take a cue from our Wise Inner Counselor, who is equally present in the material as in the spiritual. My personal experience and that of my fellow "transpersonalists" is that as we intently engage the guidance of inner wisdom, we become increasingly grounded and more able to navigate the challenges of living in the material world.

Realizing Our Intrinsic Value

Over the years I have been acquainted with some remarkable people who exhibited many of the attributes I describe as transpersonal.

Without fail, their most significant quality was their practicality which appeared to flow from an uncommon ability to "tune in" to inner guidance.

The other overriding characteristic was that of a positive self-regard that reflected a sense of personal worthiness that was balanced, generous and based on core values.

My experience shows me that this type of genuine self-worth is essential for each of us if we desire to be our True Self in any situation. And I believe it is accessible when we realize our intrinsic value and accept that we truly are lovable.

This inner shift is key to tapping into the deeper meaning of Soul Poetics and the glimmering sense of purpose which goes far beyond what we do for a living.

SELF-WORTH AS A PIVOT POINT

*Self-worth is the lever for doing your great
work and it can lead to being your True Self.*

The Need to Be Thought Worthy

Humans are social creatures. As such we have a basic need to belong
to a group of like-minded individuals and to be accepted by them.
Until we have matured psychologically, we gain much of our sense
of worth from the opinions of other group members.

However, the human heart is endowed with an inner urge to
grow, to develop, to transcend today's awarenesses and accomplishments. That urge tends to create discontentment with our current
circumstances.

As I have worked with my Wise Inner Counselor and med-
itated on this dynamic, I have noticed that a powerful shift takes
place within the sense of worthiness in people whose intention is to
transcend their former self.

Many of these individuals (myself included) also have had
peak experiences that change their outlook on themselves and on
the groups with whom they associate. My sense is that the Wise
Inner Counselor provides the impetus to continue this growth.

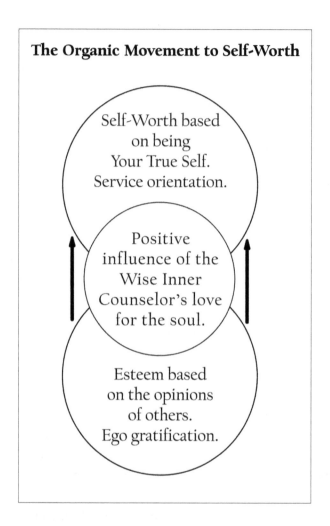

The Organic Movement to Self-Worth

Self-Worth based
on being
Your True Self.
Service orientation.

Positive
influence of the
Wise Inner
Counselor's love
for the soul.

Esteem based
on the opinions
of others.
Ego gratification.

The Organic Movement to Self-Worth

For most of us, the positive opinions of others resonate with our basic need to belong to a supportive group. Others bolster or reduce our self-esteem by what they think, say and do toward us.

If we are fortunate, however, at some point we discover that regard ringing hollow unless we honor ourselves.[20]

This shift can be a gradual process of life proving to us the shallowness of seeking external approval.

Or we may experience a sudden awakening that turns our sense of self on its head and sends us running to the unseen yet profoundly felt arms of our Wise Inner Counselor. It is this presence residing in our heart of hearts which we honor as the truth of our innermost reality.

The point is: As we pay attention to that wise voice and strive to make its subtleties more apparent, we will naturally move into the realm of real self-worth—a vital aspect of our True Self and the origin of the endeavors in life that are service-oriented rather than based on the need for ego-gratification.

Honoring the Restless Heart

A gifted instructor once said to me, "To have a breakthrough in your writing, you have to get really sick of your old self." I believe that a similar, very uncomfortable experience takes place for everyone who is striving to become their True Self.

Our hearts grow restless and unfulfilled as we discover that we no longer fit with our old crowd. We find ourselves stepping away from friends, family, colleagues and clients. We have become discontented, troubled, possibly irritated—perhaps even bored.

Suddenly, we see that the approval of the old gang is not sufficient. If we are to find our true vocation—the Soul Poetics we came to this life to accomplish—we must become Self-reliant (reliant on the True Self) and responsible for our worthiness.

We must honor ourselves. Not in the prideful sense of an inflated ego, but in the awakened sense of connection with the Love that lives in our deepest heart of hearts.

Answering the Call to Greatness

In that interval when nothing feels right, change can come. Destiny speaks, often loudly. Perhaps as an earthquake of circumstance or in the premonition of looming dire events.

Here is where the Wise Inner Counselor's call to come up

higher rings like a clarion bell, and we find ourselves compelled into action by our soul's deep longing to answer that call.

This beckoning to personal greatness flies straight to the soul like a bolt of lightning. A light shines. Contact is made. We take the hand of our True Self, and together we place our feet on the path of transcending our former self. We step off into the Great Unknown that must be faced if we are to become who we really are.

Worthiness Is an Inside Job

Self-worth based on our core values is two-fold. We are honest about our human limitations and weaknesses, while simultaneously being cognizant of our gifts, talents and capabilities.

This mature self-worth is neither boastful nor falsely humble. It instills in us a strong determination to fulfill our reason for being while admitting that we need the energy, Love and illumination of our True Self.

To have self-worth is to honor our Wise Inner Counselor—to trust that it will focus all of its faculties on the matter at hand. We hold our Self in positive regard and we expect miracles because we know where our value lies.

Healthy self-worth welcomes the magic of synchronicity that is a sure sign of the Wise Inner Counselor's presence—connecting us to the unseen life of things.

My Experience of the Process

As I have mentioned, listening to the voice of inner wisdom has saved me more than once. For those events I credit the determination of my Wise Inner Counselor who has never failed to send me guidance that was eminently practical at the exact time I needed it.

As these episodes of being rescued from potential or actual calamity continued to unfold in my life, I finally had to accept that an unseen, profoundly felt, unconditional, ever-present compassion was the impetus for this guidance.

I would experience an even greater sense of worthiness in my being every time I accepted its intercession. I believe this is when I fully determined to work with my Wise Inner Counselor.

And Here Is Where Words Fail

Trying to describe the totality of Love that flows in, through and around me in these moments is like trying to describe the scent of a forest after a rainstorm or the power of the ocean or the majesty of the mountains. You had to be there.

One of my favorite photos of Stephen and me,
taken early in our marriage as we contemplated our future
at the Maroon Bells wilderness area outside of Aspen, Colorado.

We Teach Who We Are

Several years ago I was struck by a simple, yet vital concept: We are always teaching others who and what we are by our appearance, actions, tone of voice, body language and facial expressions.

In the same way, the Wise Inner Counselor teaches who it is

by the particular energy it conveys and by the feeling we get when we are open to its intimations. The key is that we must choose to perceive its presence. When we do, our self-worth increases.

This change occurs when we become weary of relying on outer accolades—when we give up trying to please others, such as parents, bosses, friends or our concept of a disapproving god.

When we focus on our core values, the Wise Inner Counselor cuts through the noise and creates an opening for us to step into genuine self-worth.

An Example to Follow

I believe that one of the most important aspects of following the example of our True Self is for our sense of self-worth to positively affect others, encouraging them to the same experience.

Even when we are having an "off" day, if we can remember how we think, feel and behave when we are truly connected with our Wise Inner Counselor, we may soon find ourselves assuming that demeanor and projecting that same positive energy.

This is a practice I have had to learn because most of my professional life has been spent in service to the public in occupations as varied as restaurant work, self-development workshop leader and musical comedy actress. (I always considered raising the spirits of an audience as an act of service.)

I may not have realized it at the time, but I see now that when I wasn't feeling my best and still had to perform, I would summon the presence of my Wise Inner Counselor to help me act as if I were that True Self until I could feel my inner reality acting in me.

Without fail, at the conclusion of a performance or whatever work I was engaged in, I would experience a sense of fulfillment— not only of a job well done, but of a greater connection with my internal reality that boosted my self-worth.

As worthiness grew in me, the next time I needed that inner strength, I remembered to call upon it much sooner.

CREATING AN INNER BULWARK

*If we know who we are and maintain a
sense of our intrinsic value, life's most
difficult challenges will not undo us.*

Why Self-Worth Is So Important

My experience as an author and workshop presenter in the grief
counseling and life transitions community has shown me that loss
usually sends people in one of two directions.

Some will spin out, sink into anger, depression, despair,
addictions or anti-social behaviors. Others will go deep into their
souls where they find the Wise Inner Counselor who has always
been there to connect them to their true reality.

Some people lose hope, faith and purpose, while others find
reason for new hope. Their self-esteem strengthens and they discover more vital purpose that transforms the worst experience of
their life into the most important.

Consider Victor Frankl, who wrote *Man's Search for Meaning*.
He had absolutely everything taken from him except the thread of
life he hung onto amidst the horrendous circumstances of a Nazi
concentration camp. That experience taught him that he could
still retain his soul and his spiritual connection to something much

larger and more eternal than the evil that surrounded him.

Why the difference? It really comes down to the extent to which each individual soul is aligned with their highest principles, especially when life is its most challenging.

Frankl may have discovered the depth of his being in a Nazi concentration camp, but I am certain he had been building that connection—the poetics of his soul—for a very long time.

Why Not Us?

One of life's biggest lessons is when we are called to respond greatly to dramatic changes. Those "sink or swim" events compel us to rise to the occasion and do what is being asked of us.

When my husband received a diagnosis of terminal cancer, we could not help but wonder, "Why us?" We thought we were doing everything right—good diet, exercise, spiritual practice. How could cancer strike us so suddenly?

We honestly could not breathe from the shock. And yet, as we sat with this new reality, we came to a profound sense of, "Why *not* us?" If anyone had the internal and external resources to deal with life's inevitable, though too-soon end, we were those people.

So we pulled ourselves together and leaned into our spiritual practice as never before. As a result, Stephen's final months were for each of us a transformative time of deep communion and insight.

Those experiences, which were based on our willingness to embrace what life was sending us and our trust in the Wise Inner Counselor's guidance, have sustained me for more than a decade.

They have informed my way of being and have been the source of every right action I have taken since Stephen's departure from this world.

Self-Worth as a Remedy for Fear

As long as we are living in the finite realms of time and space, we are subject to our human psychology. In fact, the longer we are on the path of self-realization, the greater is the likelihood that we will find ourselves dealing with some really knotty issues that surface at the most inopportune times.

Actually, I have a feeling that inner guidance considers the timing to be perfect for us to face a behavior pattern that has plagued our soul for lifetimes. My own sense of these situations is that my Wise Inner Counselor has determined that I have developed sufficient self-worth to conquer an ancient momentum.

The lesson is to not become frightened of what we may discover in the deepest recesses of our unconscious. Our own repressed thoughts and feelings can create an aggressive subconscious that berates us in a steady stream of blaming, shaming self-talk.

We can be especially challenged to maintain our connection with inner guidance if we have been influenced by projections of hellfire and damnation from those who espouse a negative deity.

In addition, we live in a society that relentlessly pummels us with messages of deficiency—even from people who could, if they chose, be our fellow travelers on the road to soul illumination and freedom from limiting perceptions.

All of this negativity tries to convince us that we are hopelessly flawed and that, if we dig too deep, we will find our own version of Jurassic Park lying in wait to devour our very souls. That is so untrue.

When we find ourselves in the throes of these confrontations with our own unhealthy momentums (or projections from outside forces), the sense of true worthiness which we have gained can be the remedy for doubt and fear.

When we resolve to view ourselves with the unconditional positivity of our True Self, we fling open the doors of perception and call upon this steadfast presence to reveal to our outer awareness the intelligent, compassionate beings that we really are. The True Self is happy to oblige.

Reflection 23

OPENING THE WAY
TO SELF-WORTH

Every day our True Self offers opportunities
for us to accept that our contribution to life
is vital and that we are worthy of being loved.

Maintaining the Inner Connection

When we give away our personal power by relying on the opinions of others for our self-worth, one result can be a sense of injustice when those others find fault with how we are conducting our lives.

Only we can give ourselves the inner recognition we desire. Outer accolades do not suffice, even from people who assure us that we are loved unconditionally.

We are the arbiters of our self-worth. We find it by honoring our own gifts and by willingly engaging with the Wise Inner Counselor who holds our soul in unwavering positive regard.

Maintaining that inner connection is our responsibility, no matter how difficult the challenges life presents.

Our Self-Worth May Be Tested

Life on this planet is often cruel. It also is beautiful, inspiring and miraculous. We see what we bring to life. If we open our eyes to the positive as well as the negative, we can lighten our burden and that of others. The change begins at home.

If we would have justice, we must be just. If we would receive compassion, we must be compassionate. If we would end violence, we must end our own internal warring.

If we would find mercy, we must be merciful—first to ourselves, for only then can the balm of loving-kindness flow out from us to others. And most significantly, if we would have others value us, we must value ourselves.

Without that change of heart, we may harbor a belief that we are victims. Or we may indulge in human sympathy—an agreement with despair and the conviction that suffering is the only reality.

In my experience, those who are truly aligned with their Wise Inner Counselor do not want retribution or pity—no matter how dire their circumstances may be. Their sense of inner dignity keeps them from sinking below the waves of adversity.

And, still, sometimes we all need a helping hand to remember who we are.

Honoring the Humanity of All

Dame Cicely Saunders, founder of the modern hospice movement, famously said, "You matter because you are here." It warms the heart to witness how hospice honors the humanity of those who care for the dying as well as those who are exiting this world.

Being in the presence of these compassionate medical and non-medical helpers gives hope and comfort to all who receive their ministrations. Many patients actually improve when they are afforded the dignity of a living person rather than being identified by the terminal conditions from which they are suffering.

This patient-centered care can provide the dying with an opportunity to reflect upon their lives in way that allows them to realize the value their lives contributed to their own loved ones and to the world as a whole.

Persons who may have doubted their worth are then able to depart from this world knowing that they mattered because they were here.

Gratitude Provides Another Opening

A wise friend told me about a twelfth-century Tibetan Buddhist teaching that gratitude opens the way to all other positives in life. I believe this applies particularly to developing and staying grounded in a tangible, felt sense of self-worth.

I have seen this played out in my life and in the lives of others who have maintained an attitude of gratitude—even for the tough assignments the Wise Inner Counselor delivers from time to time.

For me, gratitude is the remedy for over-thinking all manner of life circumstances. I can feel the shift in my own being when I replace those old "woulda, coulda, shoulda" thoughts with a heart-felt expression of gratitude for the process of forging a wise path through my life.

Of course, it is challenging to be grateful for life's tragedies. And yet, whenever I've asked attendees of the professional development courses I have taught to identify the life lessons they were most grateful for, invariably they cited the toughest ones.

I agree. The better I have listened for inner guidance during the worse things that ever happened to me, the more rapidly have those events transformed into important opportunities for soul growth which profoundly enriched my life.

The True Self Needs Our Gratitude

One of my dear friends told me the story of how she suffered over the deaths of her brother and parents. At some point she began to realize that the things which had happened to her human self had also happened to her spiritual Self.

As she sat with her pain, feeling that Spirit can also suffer, she began to recite all of the aspects of her life for which she was grateful. After a while, her pain lifted and she felt the gratitude of her Wise Inner Counselor for her realization that Spirit had shared in her experience of loss.

My friend's adult daughter told about a similar experience with the power of gratitude. She explained that on occasion she has become depressed without realizing it. Only after observing that she has been in an emotionally dark place for some time is she able to take steps to pull herself out of the funk she has fallen into.

Her favorite remedy? Writing in her journal and speaking aloud all of the things for which she is grateful.

Worthiness and Our Soul Poetics

Our souls do have a genuine need to produce positive achievements. Excellence is an important element of our true identity.

The secret is for all of our endeavors to be inner-motivated. One way we can sense the Wise Inner Counselor's love for us is in how it helps clear obstacles to our accomplishments. It shows us how to avoid pitfalls and create novel solutions to challenges in the workplace and at home.

The excellence that results nourishes our self-worth in a practical way because the lessons we learn from both our successes and our failures prove that we are capable of doing great work. The more we listen to inner guidance and implement what we hear, our belief in our intrinsic worthiness increases.

Self-worth which flows from our alignment with the True Self gives us the courage to live within the highest principles of our Soul Poetics where being and doing weave together in the harmony of integration.

"God's Promise" by Ross Brunson

PART FIVE

Oneness in the Light of Your

Wise Inner Counselor™

Reflection 24

INTEGRATING BEING AND DOING

*Weaving the realms of being and doing leads
to selfless actions and a life well lived.*

What Does Being Integrated Feel Like?

Recently I attended a workshop during which the facilitator said, "Tell me how it feels to be in the flow of inner integration." He asked us to write out our experiences, which to me meant expressing what being congruent with my Wise Inner Counselor is like. Here is what I wrote:

> Being consciously congruent with my deepest thoughts and feelings is an exquisite, sometimes humorous, full-body experience. I feel no shame or self-consciousness. I feel spiritually connected and also connected with others. There is an enormous sense of freedom in this flow because I belong to my True Self.

Integrating our consciousness with our actions is achieved by not trying to be anything or anyone other than our True Self. When we attain such a state of internal harmony, we can feel our soul reaching down deep into the ground of our being—into the very root of what makes us most real. Immediately, we bound back up with our hearts open, ready to receive whatever emerges in our lives. In this moment we comprehend the intertwining of being and doing, which act as the warp and woof of the tapestry of our life.

Each Contains the Other

Being and doing are more than ingredients we simply stir together in a pot to create a third something into which they then disappear. They are complementary ways of operating in the material world that are always in conversation.

Each contains elements of the other so their finest execution gives the appearance of unity. Yet the two ways of living are always slightly unequal—always switching who is leading. That exchange is what gives them their dynamism.

Doing is always unfolding based on being's state of mind. And our state of mind reveals itself in what we do.

Weaving a Spiral Pattern

The dynamic of being and doing pulsates in their interaction where they weave back and forth, up and down, creating spiraling patterns of wholeness that we may only recognize after the fact.

Almost like pairs skaters whose blades carve criss-crossing lines in the ice, here is a collaboration of two wholes, equally matched in wisdom, curiosity and kindness. Their intention is to enhance the other, not compete for dominance.

Who leads is situational depending on the context and requirement of the hour. Prominence is handed back and forth, completing the day's commission, knowing that neither partner will ever be the same.

In Contemplation of Being and Doing

I often find myself contemplating this partnership. Here are a few of those musings which I offer for your meditation. I encourage you to let yourself slip into the movement of these two elements of your True Self. How do they dance or skate or weave in your life? Do these thoughts spark any resonance with your experience?

Being is communion—coming into union. Allowing myself to give full attention to the present, whether alone or with others.

Being is not always tuning in. Sometimes it is a matter of tuning out the distractions of a very noisy world—especially the idle conversation that adds nothing but static to my reception of inner guidance.

Doing is enhanced by following the spark of inspiration, even when it wakes me up at 2:00 or 3:00 or 4:00 a.m. and then again at 5:45 a.m. to tell me a secret that was hiding in plain sight.

Will We Let Ourselves Be Loved?

As we engage inner guidance in all our being and doing, we continue to develop greater levels of self-mastery. In some ways, that increased maturity makes us very aware of our remaining faults.

Fortunately, we know that our Wise Inner Counselor is also aware of those faults, but only insofar as that perception is useful in helping us overcome them. This loving presence steadfastly holds the image of our soul's reality in the absolute conviction that we are well on our way to uniting with our True Self.

The question becomes: Will we allow ourselves to be so loved that we joyously enter into the process of transcending our former self in the way that inner guidance would lead us? Extending ourselves to others can help us embrace the process.

The Power of Compassion

One of the welcome results of allowing the cycles of being and doing to weave in and around us naturally, is the growth of compassion.

The unconditional Love of the Wise Inner Counselor infuses our consciousness and elevates our responses toward others. We find ourselves focusing on people's strengths, urging them to higher purpose and facilitating their self-actualization. We remain centered in the integration of our being and doing while generously extending ourselves into situations where we can help.

Our compassion tends the home fires, yet gladly ventures out into the storm to help others negotiate solutions for the benefit of all parties.

We become fearless because our understanding of human nature is neither offended by the differences in people, nor lost in their divisiveness. The voice of Love within encourages us to accept others at their level of awareness and treat them as they would like to be treated within the context of mutual respect and positive self-regard.

Receiving the Heart of Another

The True Self knows that often just listening to what people have to say about their situation is the most compassionate action we can take. Very often others only need someone to listen, to provide a safe place for them to take risks in their own development and to witness the joy of their self-discovery.

In being present with another person's dilemma, listening to their struggles or fears, their deepest hopes and dreams, their uniquely novel ideas, we become more than merely loving. We are transfigured into Love in action.

Here Love becomes the signature of our being, informing our best doing and creating a life that is uplifting to our families, our companies and our communities.

In the end, Love transcends all of our projects, processes and plans to bring about that sublime state of awareness where all is Love and only Love—the source and goal of all our being and doing.

MEDITATION ON LOVE, LIFE AND THE POINT OF IT ALL

*Even when human plans go terribly awry,
the presence of Love makes it possible
for greater depth of soul to appear.*

What Is the Lesson?

If all the world's a stage and life a play, then the only real question may be: "Are we playing our parts well?"

We may also ask, "Are we learning our lessons? Are we helping others learn theirs? What are the lessons? Is one more important than another?"

Of course, there are many lessons. But there is usually at least one big one—the stumbling block, the enormous success, the love, the loss. The apparent disaster. The great find or contribution.

Oftentimes, we do not know what the lesson is. Others may be able to tell us while we are still alive. Some of us may only read about a certain lesson in a history book.

Life's Real Purpose

It seems to me the real purpose of life rises or falls on the matter of Love. Did we love and how truly? How completely and with how sincere a heart did we love? Are we being loving now?

Because when we love with our whole heart, all the other attributes that we associate with Love—selflessness, sacrifice, generosity, spirituality, humor, kindness—simply flow from us as part of the natural order of Love's presence.

Love cannot but extend itself. "The more I love, the more I have to give," said Juliet to her Romeo. It is that simple. The fount of Love overflows and bubbles up all the more gladly when its waters are received in gratitude.

Love's Miracle

The miracle of Love is that it casts out all that is unlike itself. And, in turn, Love fills in the empty places with itself, even as it generates its likeness where no one would have suspected that bits of it lay fallow, waiting to be watered and warmed by its radiance.

For Love is warm. It creates heat and generates life where perhaps none had been seen in ages. It nurtures smiles and laughter, and ends the day with a kiss and a hug and a sweet "good night."

If life is all a play, then Love writes the script, chooses the actors, paints the scenery and hires the musicians. When all is in place, Love gives the great revolving stage of life a giant spin and releases the players to carry on as they agreed at the beginning. But they must play their parts with as much love as they have received.

Life's Metaphorical Play in Action

Love is always present. However, it does not intervene unless someone invites reconnection with the generous inner guidance they may or may not realize they have forgotten.

Some of the actors in our metaphorical play do ask for help. It would seem that many more do not, sometimes causing the play they are in to stop. Or they are written out of the script. Their contract expires, so to speak.

The Play Is Always Changing

As actors in this drama, our lot is often to switch scenes, or change roles and costumes to create an entirely new storyline.

Sometimes we forget our lines. Or we miss our cues and exit when we should have merely turned around. At other times we may stay too long in one role that has long since ceased to serve our education in this life. Which, after all, is the point of the play.

Plays Within Plays

There is no reason not to forgive those who have wronged us. They were only playing a part for our benefit—which is an astonishing aspect of Love. It manages to engineer plays within plays that are designed to benefit every single member of the cast.

Even when human plans go terribly awry, the presence of Love makes it possible for richer connections, more profound learning, sweeter compassion and greater depth of soul to emerge.

It is in these time of extremity that players turn within for Love's assistance with more passionate intention than they may ever have summoned in their lives. Now they understand the need to transcend yesterday's affection with today's deeper insight that engenders hope in tomorrow's more infinite loving.

In such moments of grand illumination, the Wise Inner Counselor's gentle voice whispers into the heart:

Be still and know that I will not leave you comfortless, for I am your True Self. We are separate only in your limited perception, which cannot endure in my presence.

Nestle into your heart and sense how it is to be genuinely centered in the essence of your true being—which I am.

Rest here a moment. Slip into this timeless interval where mystery dwells. Plant your feet on the ground and reach for the stars—for both are yours in every hour of your existence.

SHOW ME THE JOY!

*Do you remember what it was like to be full
of life? To feel a sense of exuberant wonder?*

Embracing Life Fully

How long has it been since you felt the total exhilaration of simply
being alive? Being true to your Self can be like that.

Bonding with the Wise Inner Counselor means you are willing
to embrace life to the full—to soar to the mountaintops or explore
the valleys below, for joy can be found anywhere.

Being fully engaged in whatever you are doing evokes the
presence of joy as that sense of having your feet on the earth while
reaching for the stars, and believing you can get there.

There is a quality of awe about joy—an intensified essence
that sweeps us into the present moment with its innate vibration of
unity. For joy contains no element of separateness.

To be joyful is to experience oneness with all things. To be
connected with all that is powerful, compassionate and wise in our
world and beyond.

We experience joy as a totality whose flavor lingers long after
the meal is served and the guests have gone home. It emits an inner
"something" that fills up our soul with itself in a way that heals, as

temporary happiness cannot because it is inconstant.

Momentary merriment can be quashed by events or the harsh words of others. Our own critical self-opinion can ruin a pleasant scene. But joy is not swayed by these forces, for in joy is no room for dissimulation or doubt in one's True Self.

Nature Lives in Joy

Joy is Nature's way of being. The crocus does not doubt as it steadily pokes its head up through springtime snows. The colt does not question its existence as it gambols around its watchful mother or nurses contentedly. The child at play is simply at home, basking in her environment.

Here is the nature of the young and the young at heart. To see such sights reminds us of the inner joy that is present in all living things and encourages us to savor it.

Joy in the Midst of Striving

Whatever your occupation, your Wise Inner Counselor offers the satisfaction of a job well done, of being well spent in activities worth doing.

Like scaling a tall mountain, this joy is the full-bodied exhilaration of reaching a milestone, of achieving a goal that stretched you to your limits. This presence of the True Self leaves its mark like a tattoo on the heart that declares:

> *Today a door opened into the sublime. Take your work seriously, but not yourself. You will make mistakes, but let the cracks in your perfection be where the light shines through. Find humor in your humanity and kindness in your self-regard. For then you will be a joyful presence in the midst of all your striving.*

Catching the Joy of the True Self

Joy can be contagious. It is a vital energy that calls out to be infused into our homes and workplaces. When we catch the joy that comes from being bonded with our Wise Inner Counselor, we can transcend the doldrums, disenchantments, depressions or despairs that plague too many human activities.

I would love to see signs on bulletin boards or coffee cups in workplaces everywhere proclaiming:

Today is gonna be a good day!

In such an environment everybody digs deep, reaches high, holds out a helping hand when needed and gives their best effort to bring about results reflecting the heart of a community of work and life that never forgets its purpose is to improve the lives of others.

This is what joy feels like. You can experience it in your life at home and at work when you engage the voice of inner wisdom that lives in your heart as your Wise Inner Counselor.

Inner Joy Has No Opposite
Joy is more than fleeting moments of satisfaction. It lifts us out of the states that wound or burden the heart. It elevates our tranquil seasons to a way of being as our True Self.

This joy is dependent only upon our willingness to create an internal environment in which we may receive it—which means being open, vulnerable, curious. And surprisingly grounded.

True joy runs deep like a subterranean stream. Its waters flow clear and pure, transmuting what they touch. They raise us into a realm of being that exists beyond time and troubles.

When the joy of inner guidance fill us, tears may spring up. For its presence is too magnificent, too powerful, too full-bodied an experience for our physical form to contain. And so we weep in the awe of its presence. Tears come to cleanse us of all that is less than the vibration of joy's freedom that we long for in our heart of hearts.

Unfettered souls sing of joy. When we carry that song into our homes and workplaces, we elevate everyone and everything around us. We become the breath of fresh air, the novel perspective, the touch of kindness that acts like a balm to those whose lives may be a weight they find too hard to bear.

Filling Our Cups with Joy Is Soul Work
Watch a group of people who work together in trust and mutual respect. They radiate joy. That is the goal, the promise and the source of all our finest doing.

Joy says, "I see you. I value you. Together let's create something wonderful and send it out into the world so that others may share our joy."

Finding joy, bringing joy, daily filling our cups with joy is soul work. And the soul that is free to do so will be relentless in striving to express her own uniqueness, her own special way of radiating the elation that is her source and birthright.

A sense of drudgery kills joy. But who among us decides what is drudgery and what is fulfilling labor? That is one of the Wise Inner Counselor's mysteries. For we find what we contain, if only in minute quantities.

An assembly line is a mechanical thing, and the robotic repetition required to operate it can be soul killing, if we let it. But suppose we bring inner guidance to that line?

Suppose we approach even the most mundane tasks with a joyful attitude of engagement with our True Self and a helping hand to others.

Creating Uplifting Processes

Imagine what would happen if we created uplifting processes everywhere and let our doing flow from grateful, joyful hearts that know themselves beloved by their own True Self.

We are always teaching by example who and what we believe ourselves to be. If we were to let that belief be that we can live in communion with our Wise Inner Counselor, we could save our households, workplaces and communities.

Perhaps we could save the world.

Reflection 27

SPIRALING THROUGH SOUL POETICS

The experience of soul growth is a dynamic process.
This is the deeper meaning of Soul Poetics.

Revising My Perspective

When I first began developing the concept of Soul Poetics I equated it almost exclusively with discovering one's glimmering sense of purpose, which can also be thought of as self-actualization.

Recently my understanding of the poetics of our souls has expanded. It now includes not only our unique work in this world and how we achieve it, but also the state of our consciousness where we ask, "Will that state lead me to be Love in action?"

I have come to experience my own Soul Poetics as a process that contains and nurtures the conversation with being and doing as they continually spiral into increasingly refined stages of spiritual and psychological development.

Nature Unfolds in Spirals of Transcendence

As much as we would like to believe that we can create a world of predictable stability, the truth is that change is the norm of life in our universe. Even in spiritual realms, life is constantly in motion, expanding, growing in abundance and transcending itself in ever-more radiant spirals of being.

Observing Nature helped me understand that this is also how Soul Poetics functions. Spirals are everywhere in Nature. From the chambered nautilus to spiral nebulae, repeating geometric patterns are everywhere.

One of the best illustrations I found to explain this pattern was to watch time-lapse videos of ferns growing. Each stem begins as a tightly wound spiral that unfolds in myriad fronds, each of which contains leaves that grow in the same pattern that repeats over and over.

How the Spiral of Soul Poetics Unfolds

Our lives are made up of a continuous conversation between aspects of our being and the doing. That combination creates a third element, which is what I have long identified as joy.

I believe this is why, when I am fully engaged in the work that is mine to do in this life, I can rather quickly slip into a state of meditation on the essential beauty of my soul and my True Self.

The important point here is that being and doing are constantly informing and enhancing each other, weaving the fresh insights of joy which their interactions create.

The nature of this process of Soul Poetics is to perpetually transcend and include each previous understanding which then creates a new and more refined level of perception and stage of development. And each successive stage leads to increased bonding with our Wise Inner Counselor—the goal of all our striving.

Expanding Our Perception

As we know, our True Self is simultaneously aware of and active in both spiritual and material realms. As we fully align with that voice of Love, we can develop the same concurrent awareness.

The frequency of peak experiences and our desire for them

accelerates, not as a hankering after phenomena, but because the exquisite presence of Love causes every lesser manifestation to pale in comparison and fall away.

As those lesser manifestations are clearly revealed as inferior to the vision of our soul reality which the Wise Inner Counselor facilitates, we expand our perception of what Soul Poetics can mean to us personally.

Nothing Else Matters

When we are congruent with the voice of Love, the Wise Inner Counselor bathes us in waves of illumination that reveal new insights into our true work in the world—our Soul Poetics.

We observe how inner guidance is totally dedicated to our soul's liberation from limitation. And we realize that nothing else matters except that we become the fullness of our True Self.

Day by day our awareness of higher principles expands, which increases the quality of our work. At a certain point, we see that we are living with a foot in both material and spiritual realms.

As we become increasingly aware of our innate spirituality, we experience the tangible sensation of living in a sphere of oneness with our Wise Inner Counselor.

Those Who Live on the Spiral of Soul Poetics

I have been privileged to know a few people who have achieved this union of their humanity with their spirituality.

They could be described as self-transcenders, and I expect that many of them would acknowledge the description. They seem to be always in the flow of transcending their former selves.

In conversation these people will agree that no one's destiny is entirely secure as long as they live in the imperfect world of time and space. So they do not rest on their laurels and they do not take for granted the opportunities that life presents to them.

There is a strength of character about these individuals that shines out from a light in their eyes and a fiery spirit that holds to their own highest principles and champions what is most noble, honest, caring and genuine in others.

One way to explain what makes these people remarkable is to say that they radiate a presence that inspires us.

If our own inner sight happens to be open, we may perceive an aura of unusual brightness surrounding them.

If we are to follow them in their daily activities, we will likely observe them traveling through life illumined by inner wisdom, offering the insight they have gained and the Love they have become to a planet in desperate need of both.

We Can Follow in Their Footsteps

Seeing that others have attained union with their True Self can make us optimistic for our own journey through life. We have reason to hope, as the Wise Inner Counselor assures us that we are also made of the Love which others have embodied and for which it speaks.

That knowledge motivates us to dedicate all of our endeavors to the betterment of this life we have been given. Like thousands of self-transcenders before us, we realize that the great longing of our souls is to be Love and to find those in this world who can receive that Love which we so fervently desire to share.

We want to leave footprints of illumination that others may follow as we spiral through the Soul Poetics we came to offer and then move on to the profound depths of perception and heights of awareness into which our True Self is eager to lead us.

In this moment, we are offered a vision of a future that can be.

A Vision of Wholeness

We imagine our soul and Wise Inner Counselor as a pair of ballroom dancers. They are waltzing on a spiral staircase that winds through a magnificent tower made of iridescent, marble-like substance that glistens as if lit from within.

We see the partners perfectly united, whirling around each other as music of unspeakable ethereal beauty fills the atmosphere. With each turn of the waltz, they climb a step higher until they reach the very peak of the tower.

As we watch, the ceiling opens wide and the dancers spin up into the blazing light of universal oneness which radiates out like a sunrise that promises a grand adventure in the dawning day.

And as we listen with open hearts and minds, we hear the voice of Love urging us:

Aspire to this, aspire to this, aspire to this.

Meet me where I am and all will be well with your life.

The oneness you long for exists within and around you. All that remains undone is your acknowledgement of the truth of your being.

Reflection 28

A POEM OF THE DAWN

I am writing into the thin place of dawn,
the hour before sunrise when the
twilight of promise emerges.

Here is where inspiration is born,
where we sacralize
the day that is coming,
where we set the sail of being
to guide the course
of all our doing.

Like mariners heading for a new world,
we follow the sun,
taking a lesson from its constancy
as it faithfully shines
through all the seasons of our life.

And like the ancients and the poets
who watched from a spinning planet,
our perception is mistaken.

For we are the ones who are traveling,
whirling through our universe,
turning different faces
to catch the sun's attention,
adoring the source of life and light
that pulses in its own race through cosmos,
pulling Earth along
on the golden thread of gravity.

Helios experiences great bursts
of doing in its being,
while here on Earth
we are challenged to be present
in the ever-changing aspects of our life.

From space our watery blue sphere
appears serene,
breathtakingly fragile,
in need of tender care,
finite and yet mighty
in the infinite possibilities
its existence offers.

Suspended, held firmly in the Sun's fiery gaze,
Earth may turn her face away
in nighttime's need for rest.

But the Day Star never loses sight
of its blue bauble,
flung out from itself
in Love's unbridled affection
for manifestation.

A Bit of This and That

Notes

Acknowledgements

The Conversation Continues

The Purpose of Life

Notes

1. Cheryl Lafferty Eckl, *Reflections on Doing Your Great Work in Any Occupation* (Livingston, MT: Flying Crane Press, 2021).

2. William Wordsworth, *Lines Written a Few Miles Above Tintern Abbey, on Revisiting the Banks of the Wye during a Tour, July 13, 1798.*

3. Michael J. Gelb and Sarah Miller Caldicott, *Innovate Like Edison: The Five-Step System for Breakthrough Business Success* (New York: Penguin Group, 2007).

4. The Institute of HeartMath, *The Heartmath Solution* (New York: Harper-Collins, 1999).

5. Robyn Davidson, *Tracks* (New York: Vintage Books, 1995, 2014), p. 197.

6. Julia Cameron, *The Artist's Way: A Spiritual Path to Higher Creativity* (first published by Jeremy P. Tarcher/Putnam, 1992).

7. See Pablo Picasso at https://www.goodreads.com/author/quotes

8. Ned Herrmann, *The Creative Brain* (Lake Lure, NC: Brain Books, 1989).

9. See www.BrainGym.org for books, tapes, and CDs of the exercises.

10. O'Donohue, John, *Anam Cara: A Book of Celtic Wisdom* (New York: Harper-Collins-Perennial, 1997) p. 126.

11. Exact reproduction of Heraclitus's words varies by source, of which there are many. Here are two other versions of his famous quote:
"No man ever steps in the same river twice, for it's not the same river and he's not the same man."
"You could not step twice into the same rivers; for other waters are ever flowing on to you."

12. John O'Donohue published a gorgeous book on Beauty. These pages are my musings, inspired by his insightful work. See *Beauty: The Invisible Embrace* (New York: HarperCollins-Perennial, 2005).

13. Eckl, *Reflections on Doing Your Great Work*.

14. Eckl, *Poetics of Soul & Fire* (Livingston, MT: Flying Crane Press, 2015).

15. See Reflection 29: "When Work Becomes Sacred" in *Doing Your Great Work*, p. 143.

16. Institute of Transpersonal Psychology, now known as Sofia University, www.sofia.edu.

17. Abraham H. Maslow, *The Farther Reaches of Human Nature* (New York: Penguin Books, 1976) p. 14.

18. Eckl, *A Beautiful Death: Keeping the Promise of Love* (Livingston, MT: Flying Crane Press, 2010, 2015, 2018) p. 4-5.

19. Jack H. Engler, "Becoming Somebody and Nobody: Psychoanalysis and Buddhism," in *Paths Beyond Ego: The Transpersonal Vision*, Roger Walsh, M.D., Ph.D., and Frances Vaughan, Ph.D., eds. (Los Angeles: Jeremy P. Tarcher/Perigee, 1993), p. 119.

20. Patricia Spadaro, *Honor Yourself: The Inner Art of Giving and Receiving* (Bozeman, MT: Three Wings Press, 2009). Also available in audiobook format.

Acknowledgements

I Have Had a Lot of Help
There have been a number of instances in my life when I have felt that my soul had her own agenda and that I, in my outer awareness, just went along for the ride. I never could have predicted, or even imagined, that my future would unfold as miraculously as it has.

I have had a lot of help.

Life can be like that when we follow the promptings of our Wise Inner Counselor. Through the inevitable "thicks and thins" of a life lived with determination in the search for how inner guidance works, I have felt my soul being tutored so that one day I might realize that my True Self has been part of me every step of the way.

My heart overflows with gratitude for this extraordinary presence whose ineffable inspiration is the impetus and guidance for the insights I have offered through these reflections.

Profound thanks also to the artists whose beautiful artwork is included in this book, to my colleagues Theresa McNicholas and James Bennett, and to my dear Stephen. Life is a miracle because we are in it together.

Finally, I would like to thank you, dear reader, for your kind attention as I have shared my musings on what being your True Self can mean in any situation. This opportunity is a grace which I will always cherish.

The conversation of *Being Your True Self* continues with a companion book.

What makes your work great and you great at work?

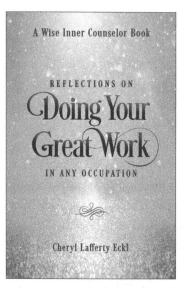

Award-winning author, poetess, life transitions facilitator and inspirational teacher Cheryl Lafferty Eckl has spent years pondering those questions.

Now, for the first time in print, she shares her reflections on the timeless principles, behaviors and attitudes that can help you become highly effective in any occupation.

Regardless of career choices, our heartfelt endeavors are where we make or break ourselves. Where we prove what we are made of. Where we share the noblest aspect of ourselves—the part that is most caring, honest, trustworthy and responsible, known as the True Self or Wise Inner Counselor™.

Cheryl invites you to unlock this wise voice of Love and find within your own heart the real secret to fulfilling your personal greatness amidst the challenges of the twenty-first century.

166 pages * ISBN: 978-1-7367123-2-0

More from the Wise Inner Counselor™

Things are different now.
Normal has changed.

There is a tension in the air, a crackling of widespread disruption that threatens to overthrow our former ways of understanding who we are and what we do.

When chaos erupts, we lose our moorings. We are not who we were and we have not become who we will be in situations that are in constant motion.

Still, in the midst of changes on a scale we have never imagined, there is a way to do more than survive.

Now you can...
Thrive Through Chaos in Every Situation

This dynamic retreat experience engages your powerful inner guidance as you find meaning, peace of mind and a way to help others navigate the rough waters of life's most dramatic transitions.

Cheryl invites you to join her in:
- Transforming coping into processing
- Engaging your Wise Inner Counselor
- Transcending your former self
- Enhancing your creativity
- Improving your problem-solving ability
- Emerging as your True Self

See www.CherylEckl.com for details.

The Purpose of Life

The purpose of life is to be Love,
to embody its unity as unspeakable joy,
to flower in Earth's garden
as a hundred thousand blooms.

Imagine putting down roots,
drinking in pure air, reaching for the sun,
being washed by morning showers,
while basking in the great presence
that simply is the essence of being
that holds us all together.

Since early childhood, Cheryl has had a zest for life. As a singer and actress, she used her dramatic and comedic skills to delight musical theater audiences across the USA.

When she turned her attention to helping others as a professional development trainer and life transitions facilitator, a new audience was equally receptive—this time to her knowledge and unique insights into life's transitions.

Cheryl has delivered her practical wisdom with intelligence, humor and real-life stories for several decades and has trained top performers in a variety of industries.

She holds a master's certificate in Transpersonal Psychology and continues to write in multiple genres from her home in Livingston, Montana, where big skies and lofty mountains inspire her life and work with her own Wise Inner Counselor.

Learn more about Cheryl's books, videos, audios, courses and retreats at www.CherylEckl.com.